KELLY W

CO-FOUNDER AND COA

CW00821658

ADAPT
GROW
THRIVE

HOW TO *SUPERCHARGE* YOUR CAREER

ADAPT GROW THRIVE

Fisher King Publishing
www.fisherkingpublishing.co.uk

Book designed by Clare Baggaley
www.clarebaggaley.graphics

www.findyourwings.co.uk

DEDICATION

Thank you to all my friends and family
for their feedback and encouragement;
especially Duncan with his unwavering
support of all my goals.

My hope is for Sam and Caitlin to realise
their huge potential as they grow up and
smash it out of the park!

FIND YOUR WINGS AND THRIVE

CONTENTS

GROW
– LOOK FOR IMPROVEMENTS

GROW: TAP INTO YOUR SUBCONSCIOUS

GROW: ASSESS ALL CHOICES

GROW: TAKE CONTROL OF YOUR WORKLOAD

GROW: BE ALERT BUT NOT PARANOID

WRAP UP

INTRODUCTION

A first step into a professional career or a fresh start in a new role can be as terrifying as it is exciting. At these times, we can all use some help. Perhaps some advice, inspiration or a practical tool would best help you, but whichever one it is, you need it to come from someone whom you trust, someone who has been there and someone who understands. So let's go on a journey together and I will accompany you every step of the way. Through this book you can tap into my twenty years of professional experience as well as my empathy and understanding from years of mentoring people in the same position. We will help you to adapt, grow and thrive in your new career.

LET ME INTRODUCE MYSELF...

I'm Kelly, your new travel companion. I'm an energetic, ambitious, creative, nurturing soul who spent twenty years working my way 'up the ladder' of the professional, corporate world. I found my strengths in marketing, digital, strategy and communication – in sectors where women were rarely seen at the boardroom table.

With every challenge I met, problem I solved and trick I learnt, I felt a strong desire to pass on that knowledge to others, hoping that it would help them navigate their own paths and use their own strengths to combat the challenges they were facing. I have mentored those starting their careers for many years, both within the organisations I worked for and for the Chartered Institute of Marketing. I find the mentoring relationship constantly rewarding, with learning going both ways. It's wonderful to see an individual that I've worked with getting an important promotion or finding success with a project they have been struggling with. Equally, I learn something new from every new person who works with me.

As a mum of two, my experience was broadened by having to juggle maternity leave, returning to work, rediscovering my identity both at home and at work, and undertaking a complete review of my priorities. I also witnessed many of the real struggles that working mums faced as senior women within large organisations built around the male work ethic.

We have to admit that the working world is not the same for men and women, so without getting too political or activist, I'll give you some facts and experiences for you to take away and digest, with the hope that you can add your own voice to the ongoing fight for equality.

WHY YOU ARE HERE

You're at the start of a whole new chapter of your life. This next journey will see you launch yourself into a new career, perhaps something you've been training for, studying for and thinking about for a long time. You've probably had some sleepless nights wondering if this is the right path for you. This transition will influence your whole life and will impact all those around you, so it's not surprising that you're a little preoccupied. You're looking for some support. Someone who can give you practical help on one hand and also reassure or challenge you on the other.

You are unique. You want to be heard, appreciated and seen for you. So, your career also needs to be personal to you. The challenge is that you also need to fit in with working culture to make progress in a business. How do you find that balance? How do you play to your strengths, chase your dreams, enjoy your job, create a balanced life, learn, listen, be both in control and seek guidance and ultimately have a career that is rewarding and successful? It's a lot, I know!

With my decades of experience and your fresh approach and exciting skills, we will take all those ideas and create a positive, solid, exciting career foundation which will allow you to thrive, while giving you tips on preparing for and tackling some of the more common challenges that you'll undoubtedly face.

I understand that even in a job you enjoy there are

times when it feels like you're hitting hurdles, feeling overworked, stressed and under-appreciated. This is where my experience can help. By noticing these triggers early, you'll learn how to tackle them and build resilience which will serve you well throughout your career.

I'll give you a very honest and practical guide built on twenty years of 'walking the walk', with lots of lived examples. We'll look at how to create longer-term goals to keep you focused and energised, while providing a guiding light on the bad days. We'll explore the attitudes and skills that will best serve you, as well as ways to tackle a variety of day-to-day situations; including how to say 'no', how and when to stand your ground, how to take responsibility for your own development and how to promote yourself in a way that feels comfortable to you.

I want you to have a successful, healthy career and that is a core aim of this book; a career which is sustainable and good for you mentally and physically, as well as being rewarding and exciting.

HOW THIS ALL WORKS

We're going to be using a fictional journey along a river to chart our progress through the stages of your career. You are at the helm of a boat. It can be any boat you like, but you have to be able to manage it alone. When I think of my boat, I imagine that I'm in a canoe-style vessel with a long oar which I can use to either paddle standing up or sitting in the bottom. It is silent and can be moved easily, both by me and by outside influences, so learning how to handle it and read my surroundings are critical. Its quiet nature also allows me to appreciate the calm, gentle times with no interruptions. It is both my transport and my teacher. What does your boat look like?

We will tackle each section of the river in short bursts and after each story section, we will come back to the real world and explore how the twists and turns we've faced along the river relate back to our daily working lives. I'll be asking you to get involved and do some exercises as we go along to help you reflect on the skills and knowledge we've learnt and how to apply them. At the end of each section is a practical list of tips which you can apply today and can keep coming back to whenever you feel stuck.

The whole journey is split into three sections: **ADAPT**, **GROW** and **THRIVE**.

ADAPT: This is the phase at the start of a new career when you are adapting to the new environment in which you find yourself. You'll likely be seen as 'new' and therefore hopefully given the support and time needed to learn and process your new role, and how your position fits into the wider picture of the business. It is a time of adjustment but importantly the demands on you at this point are fairly minimal so you can take advantage of this too.

GROW: Once you've been in your role for a while, the Grow phase of your career is all about consolidating what you know, facing new challenges and building your resilience. A term I quite like is 'The Messy Middle', because you'll find yourself being pulled in different directions and questioning yourself one week and then having some wonderful experiences and enjoying every minute the next!

THRIVE: The THRIVE stage is all about pulling on your big pants and standing tall with your shoulders back and your head held high. By this point you'll have been working in your chosen career for a while and it will be feeling more natural: you'll have confidence in yourself and your abilities. You'll have set up some positive, sustainable routines and behaviours which give you the energy, focus, resilience and humility you need to manage most situations that are thrown at you. You'll be crushing it!

But this isn't the end game! There are still challenges to face, decisions to make and skills to learn. The stakes get higher as you get further along your journey, but you're also better equipped to deal with them. It's now important to lead in a responsible and empathetic way, paying it forward and thinking about how to support those around you at all levels.

YOUR GUIDING PRINCIPLES

As we move through our journey, you'll notice that there are three Guiding Principles which are repeated at every stage. These are the three most important 'take-aways' as they apply to any situation, no matter what stage you're at in your career or where you find yourself. If you're stuck, they are your go-to reference and they are reflected in the exercises that we practise at the end of every chapter. These are:

Guiding Principle 1: Take Responsibility
Your career is your responsibility: no one can live

it for you. You are an individual. When people look at you, they can either see an outline of a person, filled with other people's opinions and ideas or they can see YOU, a person with unique skills, passions, opinions and flaws. You are responsible for shaping what they see and being proud of it.

You are ambitious. You want promotion and recognition. You want to reach your goal. The only way to do that is to take responsibility for who you are, what you do (and what you don't do) and what you say (and don't say!). Make it easy to say, 'I did that because...' or 'I believe this is the right course of action because...' It shows integrity, bravery, insight and passion to genuinely follow your own beliefs and others will notice and respect that.

Guiding Principle 2: Show Empathy

Psychologists say that empathy is a skill that grows with age and experience. We are biologically selfish as children, caring only for what directly affects us; we don't have the mental capacity when we're young to put ourselves in the shoes of others. It's a survival technique retained from our ancient roots. But even as adults the focus is often on 'me'. How does this decision affect ME? How can 'I' get the best out of this? What did 'I' do to make that person react like that? Although we are programmed to react like this to a certain extent, focusing solely on this insular, self-centred view of the world will only get you so far.

As those of you who follow, or are involved in, any level of professional or semi-professional sport will know, no one 'makes it' alone. Even individual athletes, such as golfers, swimmers, cyclists and sprinters always credit their coaches, managers, training partners and a long list of others as a critical part of their success.

When a number of people come together and combine their expert knowledge to achieve a goal, they significantly increase the odds of winning against a person doing it alone – and they tend to have more fun along the way too. Then on 'competition day' every person wins, not just the one with the trophy.

Whilst it is important to have an eye on your own goals, feelings and needs, as humans we operate best within a group. By helping each other, everyone benefits from the collective effort and we all rise together.

Guiding Principle 3: Know Yourself
Think back to Frank Sinatra with *My Way* and you can appreciate just how long we've been hearing songs that preach about living a life that's true to ourselves. You might sing along and smile – but how well do you actually know yourself? How often do you check in to see which of your activities really give you a buzz? When did you last feel excited by a work task or feel that it was pushing you to develop a skill that you love? How well do you know and appreciate your strengths and weaknesses and how do you use them?

Getting to really know yourself honestly is a game-changer. It gives you a guiding light when you've got a hard decision to make and allows you to tap into a deeper source of energy when needed. It also brings satisfaction and contentment because you are living the real 'you'.

We'll be covering these three basic principles in more detail as we continue on our journey.

ADAPT

- LET'S GET STARTED

Picture yourself in the boat you imagined earlier. You're happily paddling along a gentle stretch of river with a light current, on a calm, warm day. You can see a good way down the river and on the distant horizon you see a beautiful palace on a hill. This is your destination; your goal or a career highpoint you want to achieve.

You have spotted the churning water of some rapids a little way ahead, and off to the sides of the river there are a couple of smaller tributary streams. But you feel prepared. You have some experience skippering the boat and understand that you'll be meeting a few challenges up ahead on your way to the palace.

However, things are never as straightforward as they seem, are they? Unbeknownst to you, beyond the rapids and behind some trees, hidden from your current view, the river makes an abrupt turn to the left and continues in almost the opposite direction to the one you're following, away from the palace. At that point, the real adventure will begin! But for now, you're unaware of this impending redirection and you're still following the straight, steady channel with your destination clearly in sight.

You notice while you're sitting in your boat that you're

still moving. There's a slow, steady pace provided by the river current, which requires virtually no effort from you. You realise that this means even when you're doing nothing, you can progress gradually towards your goal and it's a relaxing and pleasant journey. You think about this while you lazily continue your journey.

Many people decide that this type of career journey is all they need, letting the river take them at its own pace, vaguely keeping an eye out for any obvious hazards. They have some level of control over the boat, but the river is doing all the work. They only really get involved when they find themselves in the middle of some rapids that they hadn't spotted and there is some urgent, panicked paddling needed to keep afloat.

We all know people who journey through their career in this way and many of them will say that they just want to see what comes up and will deal with situations as they occur. It's great that this approach works for them and it's also worth mentioning that we can all have periods in our working lives when we want and/or need to choose this option, letting ourselves drift for a short time. This is perfectly understandable and can be of great benefit if we do it mindfully and fully appreciate this loosening of control.

However, if you're reading this book, you're probably not a good passenger. You don't want to be passively watching your career – you want to be steering that boat with precision and intent, fully alert and as prepared as you can be. I understand. I'm the same and I'm going to be with you, giving you the skills to help steer your boat in a more focused way. Let's progress to the next stage of your journey...

ADAPT: ASSESS YOUR ENVIRONMENT

You're in your boat. You've got set up and although you're still mastering the finer points of steering, you've got a good, reliable grasp of the basics. Although you are alone in the boat, that doesn't mean that you're short of conversation; your brain and your heart offer you constant advice. Their often-contradictory comments help you weigh up a sensible, risk-averse, considered view of a situation (your brain) against the emotional, empathetic option that is offering exhilaration and excitement (your heart). You're quite used to these constant companions and appreciate their insights, even if at times their differing views can tie you up in knots. In these cases, decision making is never easy. You're certain that this boat ride will give them plenty to be vocal about!

You're enjoying this new river and you allow yourself time to look around, take in the scenery and smile. You've worked hard to get here and you allow yourself some peaceful moments to reflect on how far you've already come, whilst acknowledging that you're still at the start and there's a long way to go. You tune into your brain and your heart for the first time to see what they have to say. It turns out that both are feeling quite smug about the decisions they've made so far – it all seems to be going rather well!

Looking ahead you can see some gentle bends in the river and a couple of smaller streams that feed into it. Both of these will need a little concentration when you get there, as they will disturb the water and could cause some unsteadiness in the boat. For the time being, though, you're not too concerned as they appear manageable, and you've got enough experience for these situations.

Your gaze drifts above the river and towards the horizon. In the shimmering sunlight you see your palace, high above the river, beautiful and alluring. You feel your whole body react with excitement and anticipation. Your brain and your heart both know what it means to them. By closing your eyes for an instant, you can picture yourself walking into this incredible space, feeling confident, content and calm. It's yours. Although it is far away, you can see how the river before you twists and turns into the distance and you're confident that you're on the right course. With some time, energy and determination you are certain you'll get to the palace.

Back in the boat, you feel the turbulence from the first stream start to affect your balance. You snap out of your daydream and concentrate on keeping your weight central. You take careful, precise strokes, looking around for any other dangers and push strongly through to the calm waters on the other side.

You are pleased with your success but don't have long to enjoy it as the river starts to bend gently first to the right, then to the left. Your manoeuvring skills are pretty good, so with a bit of focus you slide around these corners safely.

Just up ahead, some rapids come into view. You can't quite tell how long they go on for but the angry, white-water foaming over the rocks confirms that they are going to demand some new skills. You feel your stomach knot and your body tense. Your brain is screaming at you: *"Please, please, please – let's avoid a scary, cold, watery death at the hands of these rapids. Go another way!!"* Your brain can be a little dramatic. This would be your first proper challenge, but perhaps there is another way?

Out of the corner of your eye you notice a large stream joining yours just before the rapids. Its calm surface promises an easy ride, one where you could lie down for a while on your back in the boat and watch the clouds float by. Your brain is very approving of this potential new route. It looks so appealing and you spend a few moments assessing this new stream, trying to pick up on as many details as possible. Surely it can't be as easy as it seems…?

You notice that a few hundred metres further down it veers off sharply towards the right, in completely the opposite direction to the one you're currently following, away from your palace. Thank goodness you just spotted that detail just in time. In spite of the draw of this calm, gentle option, your heart tells you that it's not going to take you where you want to go. So, with a determined grip on your paddle, you hold steady (ignoring the butterflies in your stomach which make you feel slightly sick) and prepare for the rapids. Your brain sighs, resigned, and waits for the 'I told you so moment' that it's sure is coming.

This first part of your boat journey mirrors the early days of a career in a new business. You come to it with some limited experience, lots of confidence and a goal in sight. This stage is all about ADAPTING to your new environment; understanding how you fit in, seeing where you can add value and learning as you go.

Generally, the first few months will allow you to find your feet and in most cases, you won't be tested a great deal. A couple of small challenges, perhaps a presentation on a project or speaking at a large meeting may come up, but you've enough experience to cope and usually you'll have some notice and time to prepare.

It's in these months that you'll also start to get a sense of the real company that you've joined; its culture, its scale, its policies, your colleagues, the structure, etc. You'll quickly start noting things that you like and things that you don't. The scale and complexity of achieving your career goal, as well as a possible path to it, may begin to get a little clearer.

You may still have alerts on your social feeds for new jobs or a friend who knew that you were looking for a new challenge sends you leads. It's not unusual to be tempted by a seemingly easier job, just like the attraction of the calmer, smaller river you just encountered in your boat. But think back to your initial drive and ambition, these will help to hold you firmly on course and prepare you for your next challenge.

ADAPT: EXERCISE 1

This is a good point to take a few minutes and reflect on your career to date.

★ What was your path to your current role?

★ What have you learnt along the way, about yourself and about what you want for the future?

★ What big challenges have you already faced which you

could take something from and use in the future?

★ What's the culture like in your business? How does the structure work? Where do you fit in the bigger scheme? How do you 'get things done'? What don't you like about working there?

★ What do you see as your logical next step?

ADAPT: CREATE YOUR PALACE

The palace in our story represents a significant goal in your career development. You can steer a more focused course towards your goals if you have a clear picture of what your life will be like when you have achieved them. The easiest way to think of it is to say: *When I become a <insert type of job or specific job title> I will look like this, do this, work like this, socialise like this, live like this.* An example would be:

> When I become an IT Director, I will have a job where I make strategic decisions and inspire others to want to join me. I will be an expert in IT systems integration and will work internationally, leading teams in best-practice and talking at conferences. I will live in an industrial, loft-style penthouse apartment and be financially comfortable. I will be healthy and fitness will play an important role in my day.

The aim is not to turn you into something you're not, it's more about focusing on a version of you which motivates you. It doesn't have to be a long way into the future either. You could choose a job role which sees you going from being within a team to managing it, or the one where you are chosen to join a growing team in Australia.

It's not always easy to decide on a future persona for a career goal – sometimes it's not easy to even decide what to have for dinner tonight, so something like a career goal can seem daunting, unrealistic or unnecessary. But it's worth spending some time at the start of your journey thinking about where you are heading. I'm specifically asking you to focus on the job of the person that you'd like to become, rather than just an arbitrary goal because we associate much more easily with a type of human than just a 'thing' we want. For example, it's fairly easy to imagine a marketing director, but much harder to put specifics around a more general goal such as, 'I want to manage a team and be in charge of strategy'. Your future self can be given characteristics, habits, a full-colour life and you can find examples and inspiration in the people you see around you.

The reason that we plan at all is because having a goal makes life easier than not having one. Think of this: how much easier would it be to decide what you want for dinner one evening if you had spent fifteen minutes on Sunday planning your meals for the week? By taking some time when you're calm, unhurried and not hungry to think about meals, you can consider what you've got in the freezer, what time you'll be home each day, how many people will be eating, what else you've eaten, what you're able to cook and what food you'd like to eat. It means that you go into that week with a plan. It could be a highly detailed plan with specific meals on each day and a shopping list or it could be a vague list of dishes that you could rustle up out of what you have.

Either way, when you're hungry, tired and just want some dinner on a Tuesday night, it makes that decision process much easier and quicker. By planning and setting a goal, you've removed all the stress and time-wasting involved in indecision and the possible bad result that comes out of pressured decision-making.

Interestingly, by having a plan you also get more scope to deviate from it. When you DO have the energy and desire to have something different for dinner, you can. You could try a new recipe or go out and eat, because you know that you have the fallback option that you'd planned for originally.

It's not so hard to transfer this to your career plan. For some, their goal persona is easy to pin down and they can describe it in technicolour. They want to be a financial director with international travel, a company car and the ability to make high-level decisions that influence the direction of a whole business. For others, the goal of their career is more holistic: they have philanthropic or charitable cause that they are very passionate about and so their focus is on building awareness, driving change and making a positive impact.

It's worth pointing out here that your goal persona can (and most likely will) change as you move forward. It's ok to get so far and then realise you want something different. Nothing in life is ever wasted: everything is a building block towards your future, even if you don't see it straight away. So don't ever regret making a decision or taking an action – you never know how or when it may help you.

The aim of this book is just to get you off the starting blocks so that you have something to give you focus.

Try the answering the questions in the exercise below to help you flesh out a goal persona for yourself. Notice that I don't ask you what your passion in life is! Your job doesn't have to be your passion. I'll repeat that because it's important and because many people get very distracted by this notion: **Your job doesn't have to be your passion.**

You can feel happy, fulfilled, challenged and excited by a role that you're really good at, which brings out your best qualities and which you're willing to work hard at. It's just not possible for everyone to have a career by following their passion, as much as social-media influencers would have us believe otherwise. But it is possible to love being good at something and be energised by your contribution to an organisation. Develop your passion on the side and explore its potential if it feels right, but don't get obsessed by it being your only career option.

There are only seven questions in the exercise below and you may think that this seems too simplistic for such a critical decision, but that is the point of the task. Really take notice of how your mind and body instinctively react to the questions. Are there some questions which you don't want to answer or which you think are silly? Dig into your reactions a little deeper and try to peel them back and look for the 'why'.

Also, raise a little mental flag when your thoughts are straying into 'should' territory. This is when your sentences start, '*I should do this because...*' 'Should' can be a strong indicator that you're doing something for someone else; perhaps your parents' expectations are front of mind or because you're following a similar path to your friends. Keep this process true to you. The way to get to your palace is with a strong foundation that you really believe in.

Once you've got your core goal persona, you can shape it like the meal planning – it can be as complex or as vague as you like – but the important part is to HAVE a plan. Your palace will give you a compass point around which you can make decisions. It gives you the freedom to try new things, because you know that you can always come back to it. It will also help you weather the uncertain times because you can see the bigger picture and won't get lost in any short-term unhappiness. Crucially, it frees your brain from the anxiety of indecision and uncertainty, which are the quickest paths to stress and overwhelm. It's also important to remember that your palace can adapt over time, it can grow extensions or even morph into a spaceship, but it needs to exist first.

ADAPT: EXERCISE 2

Try answering these questions to help you create your own 'palace' or goal persona:

1. What are you good at; what are your strongest qualities and skills?

2. What do you enjoy doing, to the point that you'd be willing to work at it for long hours or over an extended period of time? If nothing comes to mind, then what did you used to like doing as a child? This can be a good place to start.

3. What do you definitely NOT want to do?

4. What do you enjoy about working in general and rank them in order, eg. Do you find the sector really interesting? Do you love the continuous learning and challenge? Do you feel that you make a difference in some way? Do you love working in teams with people? Are you highly motivated by the salary and perks?

5. What are the biggest downsides to work? Rank them in order.

6. What does your goal job persona do? Describe them. What are their habits? What are their strengths? What does their life look like?

7. Where are the similarities and differences between your answers to Qs1-5 and your description in Q6? What areas are do you already have a head-start in and which ones are completely new to you?

Try finishing this sentence:
I want to be a [job role]. My main priorities in my work are [insert priorities]. I judge success by [insert values]. I want to be a [job role] because…

At the end of this exercise, a clear picture of your goal persona should be emerging. It should be someone who you can associate with, who does all the things you like about work and minimises time spent doing the things you don't. Hopefully you can also start to see how your current career and plans could align to this future goal.

Congratulations! You now have a palace and a more realistic idea of your own river that will lead you there!

With that established, let's jump back into our boat.

ADAPT: LEARN TO REFLECT

You've decided that this river is where you want to be, much to the despair of your risk-averse brain, so tackling the upcoming rapids is your next priority. You look around for anything that could help you and realise that as it's the start of your journey, you haven't really picked anything up yet. You've got a life jacket, which you put on quickly, but there's nothing else in the boat. You'll have to rely on your own skills and knowledge to get you through.

As the rapids come closer, the boat starts to respond to the choppy waters and you have to alter your position to stop yourself being thrown into the bottom of the boat. You try to ignore your brain screaming obscenities at you for being so 'reckless' and focus on the quieter voice of your heart, telling you that 'you've got this'.

With a stronger stance, you focus on each twist and turn in the river, concentrating on how the flow of the water is showing you the hidden rocks. The noise of the swirling, crashing water is deafening. It drowns out any other thoughts and your focus narrows to tunnel vision – all you can see are the rapids.

The boat has sped up and you're having to make quick decisions as the dangers of the river change before your eyes every few seconds. Every fibre of your body is tense and alive, focusing 100% effort on getting you through. Your brain and your heart are silent with concentration.

After your initial shock and panic, you realise that you're actually doing well, and even starting to enjoy the experience. You are now reading the rapids with speed and accuracy and enjoying the thrill of learning to navigate as you go. Your heart is pounding as much through adrenaline and enjoyment as through exertion. You can feel it give an enormous, jubilant, 'Whoopee!'

Thankfully, 50m up ahead you see the water flatten out and you know you've almost made it. With a last push of confident steering, you explode out of the rapids. The loss of momentum is instant as the now-gentle current absorbs your energy and renders you virtually still. You stand frozen for a few moments, holding your breath as your senses return and your body begins to relax. Your brain is sulking at having been proven wrong, although secretly it's hugely relieved.

After a few moments, you can now appreciate that you're floating on a beautiful, picturesque lake. The current gently nudges you forward but there are plenty of spots where the shore is visible at the water's edge and you direct the boat over to one of the bays for a rest.

Your heart and your brain are both lulled by the surrounding beauty and peace. With the boat secured, you lie back in the bottom, gaze at the sky and reflect on what you've just been through, how it felt and what you've learnt. You replay the rapids in your mind, mentally correcting errors you made and cementing your new skills into your brain. Even in your relaxed state, the memory of the physical exertion and the adrenaline makes your heart start to race again. It was a powerful experience.

The next time you hit rapids you know you'll be prepared – more experienced and ready to enjoy it. Your brain groans at the idea of a next time, whilst your heart sings happily in the background.

We are often faced with a significant task in the early months of a new job or new career direction. It can initially appear overwhelming and scary as you'll have lots of 'firsts' to overcome, but there's a side of you which is also hungry to get going and relishing the challenge. You'll probably face it with a mix of both caution and excitement. Just like the first set of rapids, it will often be a task which pushes you a little out of your comfort zone, but for which your previous experience and skills have prepared you.

Let's take the planning of a customer event as an example. At this point, you'll have few resources to help you. The life jacket is your line manager, who should always be there to stop you drowning, should it come to that! Apart from his/her support, you'll probably need to work it all out on your own.

This is usually terrifying and exhilarating in equal measure. As the event gets closer, you'll become completely absorbed by it, with work often spilling into your personal time. But for all the long hours and hard work, you get the rewards of building your network, learning more about the company, working with new people, honing skills you already had and trying some new ones.

There are some specific skills that will start to come in handy:

★ You'll need persuasion to convince others to help you, support you and do things for you.

★ Compromise will be needed when objections or obstacles start to appear; either due to people's opinions or practical considerations for the event.

★ Two incredibly useful skills in these situations are lateral-thinking and creative problem-solving as there will always be unforeseen and/or last-minute changes which need to be made and being able to think on your feet will often save the day.

★ The final critical skill is team-working, because you'll never pull off a successful event with your sanity intact if are working alone. It's useful to take a step back and think about what team you need to make your event go smoothly and the role that you play within it.

Just like you needed a variety of skills to steer your boat successfully, a work project is a complex combination of skills, people and behaviours all working in sync.

It's important to remember to enjoy the project journey as well as look forward to the completion of it. Thriving in corporate life is about learning to find the thrill within the day-to-day. Feeling out of your depth or continually being challenged can be an incredibly rich time for you to learn new skills, improve your resilience and prove yourself (as much to yourself as to those around you). Try to find the positives hidden within the hard work – it gives a totally new perspective and makes it much more enjoyable. Finding enjoyment and satisfaction in what you do is one of the best ways to keep stress at bay and build a healthy career.

At the start I introduced our Guiding Principles: Take Responsibility, Show Empathy and Know Yourself. Here we see all three in action:

Take Responsibility
As long as the event happens and your project sponsor is satisfied, then the order in which you did the tasks or how you got them completed won't be in question. Use that flexibility to organise yourself in a way that brings out the best in you and allows you to get maximum benefit from it. By taking responsibility for what tasks you do (and which you delegate or outsource), when you do the work, how you manage the project and how and what you communicate to the business, you can focus on demonstrating your strengths and getting help where you need it. The best work project should enable you to grow and develop as well as deliver a great business outcome.

During the event itself, it's completely normal that

unexpected things will happen. This is when you can switch into problem-solving mode and tackle each issue as it arises. Don't try to predict the future, don't worry about 'what if' or what someone else may have done – use your own skills and intuition and have faith in your decisions.

It's not always about solving problems on your own either, it's about taking responsibility for your decisions, whether that be asking for help, ordering a new widget or delegating a task. It will likely be exhausting and demanding, but the end is in sight so tap into some resilience and get the job done well.

Remember to take responsibility for your own story. It's often possible to turn a negative situation or a bad decision into an opportunity and there should be lots of occasions for you to demonstrate your skills and uniqueness to stand out or to prove how capable you are. Make it work for you.

Show Empathy
This is particularly important in stressful scenarios, mainly because it can be one of the first things to go out of the window when things 'just need to get done'. If you are feeling the pressure of being on a deadline or producing something important, then others will be feeling it too, either for the same reasons or for their own project. Try to remember that you only ever see a small slither of anyone else's life, so regardless of any pressure you are feeling, it's best not to judge others. When someone goes out of their way to help you, be sure to acknowledge their kindness and model the same behaviour yourself.

Know Yourself

You need to home-in on what you're good and not so good at and what you do and don't enjoy doing. We'll do a little more work on this shortly, but for now, think of a couple of examples of each which pop into your head. The aim of the ADAPT phase is to try to do as many of things you're good at as you can and use them to balance out the less enjoyable tasks. For instance, if you love being creative and hate working with figures, then make sure you book in some time with a colleague who can help you with the budget and then follow that up with some time spent designing artwork for the event.

The immediate days after the event will feel a little unreal and your brain will be tired but still turning over everything that happened. You won't have much capacity for other work so tune into what your body is telling you and listen. This is such a core component of healthy career – pushing relentlessly onto the next thing with no break is the quickest way to stress and burnout.

Something that I learnt very late in my career, and I wish I'd known about sooner, was the value of stopping and reflecting. Just as you did in the boat, take time to look around at the lake, look back at the rapids and give your body and brain a chance to catch up and absorb what you've achieved and learnt.

There's a biological reason for doing this too. When we are operating in high-performance mode, reacting quickly, making decisions and working long hours, our body is helping to sustain this effort by flooding our system with two hormones: cortisol and adrenaline. These help to push vital nutrients and energy to our core systems, increase blood flow and ramp up our body's production of glucose sugar to help repair any damaged tissue (more useful in ancient times when running away from a lion attack could result in injury, but nonetheless we are still programmed to respond in this way). For the short-term energy and performance boost they give, these hormones do a great job, but if we keep their levels high for too long, they put a huge strain on our bodies and can have long-term health implications. By relaxing and reflecting, we are giving our body chance to take itself down a gear and reset our hormones to a normal level.

Everyone will recuperate in different ways and that's why you can either pull your boat over to the side and take a break (a day off or a holiday) or you can let the gentle current float you around the lake by going back to some easy admin tasks, filing, report writing – whatever is appropriate for your job. The key here is to reflect.

Some businesses are good at always having a 'lessons learnt' session after a project but they often focus on failures or problems during the task. While it is a great idea to dissect why things have gone wrong with a view to preventing them from happening again, organisations very rarely consider why things have gone right. What they should also be asking is, what was it about the situation, the people, the planning and the execution which came together so well to create such a success?

When starting out on some reflecting yourself, the questions below can be used as a prompt to help you explore what you did well personally and where you can improve. By understanding, or at least noting, the conditions that help you perform to your best you have a better chance of being able to replicate them next time. You are taking responsibility for your own optimum performance.

You also need to celebrate and enjoy the wins! Both your brain and your heart will thank you for some lightness and happiness to offset your mental and physical efforts. You need rewards, big and small, to help you maintain your energy levels and your overall focus. You only live once, so you need to congratulate yourself and enjoy it when things go well.

ADAPT: EXERCISE 3

Try answering these questions about a recent significant piece of work or challenge:

★ What did I do that I was most proud of?

★ What pushed me outside of my comfort zone the most?

★ Where could I have done something differently or made improvements?

★ How did I handle the problems?

★ How did I feel at the highest point?

★ How did I feel at the lowest point?

★ How did I expand my network?

★ What did I learn?

★ How did I celebrate the win?

GUIDING PRINCIPLES DEEP DIVE 1: TAKE RESPONSIBILITY

In each of the ADAPT, GROW, THRIVE sections we'll do a Deep Dive into one of the Guiding Principles to demonstrate their significance and understand them in greater detail. As we're resting and reflecting on a calm lake at the moment, it seems like a good opportunity to take a look at the first of the three: Taking Responsibility.

Your career is your responsibility. That is both a powerful concept and an intimidating one. It is powerful in the sense that this attitude can train your mind into seeing all the other river channels, tributaries and off-shoots that are accessible to you. It means that you are no longer waiting for a senior manager to suggest what your next move should be, instead you can take control and navigate in the direction that you choose. Suddenly, the options open up and you can be spoilt for choice.

This is also where it can become intimidating because it can be difficult to know how to sort and prioritise all the possibilities. How do you know which route will be best for you and what happens if you make a mistake or regret a decision? Don't panic, we'll be addressing all these ideas slowly and thoroughly in this book to give you the confidence you need to take responsibility of your career.

It's worth pointing out that your decisions may not always align with the expectations or hopes of those around you. You will also have to learn the skills of:

★ **Negotiation:** When you want to take on a new project at work to demonstrate a particular skill but need someone to take something off you to enable you to have the time, you'll need to negotiate. **THINK:** What's in it for them?

★ **Compromise:** When your manager needs you to complete something by an unrealistic deadline, you'll need to compromise on a more achievable date. **THINK:** What is the factor that's pushing your manager for their date; An event? A promise they have made? Another action finishing? By understanding this you can often find a way to keep them happy AND relieve the pressure on you.

★ **Persuasion:** You need support from someone who has something that you don't (skill, knowledge, contacts, location, etc) so persuasion is going to be key to getting them on board. **THINK:** What can I offer them in return? How could I be useful to them?

★ **Humility:** You are the captain of your own life and the responsibility for paddling your boat lies squarely with you, which means you will have very clear ideas on those things which are priorities and those which are less important. However, it's very rare that someone else will have exactly the same views as you, because no one can have identical priorities in all areas of their life, we are all individual. Remember that you are the only the centre of your own world, you're not the centre of anyone else's and you can't possibly understand all the complex nuances of another person's situation, decisions or opinions. This doesn't mean that others won't want to help and work with you, quite the opposite, but don't take this support for granted. Being respectful of and humble with those around you will help build strong, reciprocal relationships. **THINK:** Support from this person would be appreciated but isn't a guarantee, so what's my plan B?

Building these skills into your 'Taking Responsibility' career toolkit from the start will always serve you well.

Here are some practical tips on how you bring this principle to life in your daily working life:

Be confident in voicing your opinions
There have been occasions when I've not spoken out and gone with a popular or easy consensus rather than what I believed to be true. Often in these cases, something went wrong and it was very hard to then justify why I approved that original course of action. Sometimes, someone else voiced exactly what was in my head and I was left feeling that I had missed an opportunity, that someone else was now getting the credit for my good idea.

Here's one example. I was managing a new website and some creative design work had been commissioned for it. Design is always VERY subjective and you'll never get everyone to agree exactly on a way forward, but if you try to accommodate too many people's opinions the end result is often bland. I felt that the proposed design was a classic example of trying to please too many people – it was boring and unimaginative. However, it did do what we needed it to do as a website and our customer base was quite traditional and 'expected' certain things of our website. I was also not the core age-range of the intended users. But I still didn't like it!

I believed that there must be a way that we could appeal to our users AND push the design further, to engage with a younger and more digitally savvy audience to help expand the appeal of our very traditional brand. But I said nothing. Unfortunately, I didn't have the courage to voice my reservations and instead, pointed out the areas where the design did what we needed it to do; it was at least functional. No other opinions were voiced (everyone seemed to find something they liked about it) but crucially no one was shouting from the rooftops about how much they loved it either. In hindsight, this is what I should have picked up on. Anything creative should evoke a reaction, either negative or positive, because it connects with you in some way. A design which has everyone reaching for their phone to check their email, has failed.

The designs were sent out to a wider audience and I remained silent. Almost instantly, one of the marketing directors came back, horrified. She was stunned that as a project team we were so unimaginative and had demanded so little of the website design. As a global brand, albeit a traditional one, we should have been pushing boundaries and being innovative, while still retaining the link to our roots. She cited examples of design that we should be trying to emulate: the likes of Apple, BMW and others, which succeeded so well in highlighting their products, showcasing their brands.

I was mortified. I felt the same but no one else knew as I hadn't voiced my thoughts at any point. It turned out that the rest of the team were also interested in going further and being braver with the design but hadn't known where to start. Had I have spoken up earlier on, I could have led a much bolder, innovative design concept with the confidence that we could carry it off. I would have been noticed for my straight talking, my confidence in my own opinions and the ability to create something impressive. As it was, I just had to take the criticism and go back to the agency with a new brief – one now driven and owned by someone else.

After that day, I never endorsed anything that I wasn't 100% happy with and always spoke my mind. Even if my ideas weren't the ones which were taken forward, I was content that I had given my views and could always stand by them.

Whenever I have made a difficult decision – reversed an action or spoken against the majority view – only one of two things happened. It was registered but ignored (in which case there was no change to the original course of action anyway) or it made an impact and something was changed. The worst-case scenario isn't all that bad and aside from a little frustration, there's no damage done. The best-case scenario is that you make a positive difference and your colleagues listen to you.

Do your research

Confidence in your views and actions can only come from a level of certainty that what you're standing for is, in fact, the truth. If your project or action is particularly high-profile, then try to be the most informed person in the room about your decision.

Depending on the situation, this could be a quick Google search or it could be a more in-depth piece of work, but any credibility gained from standing up for your actions will very quickly be dissolved if your colleagues find out that you've misled them (intentionally or otherwise). Always make sure that you have enough information to back up your views and always be truthful if your evidence falls short or turns out not to be as expected.

Research your colleagues too. What are their opinions on what you're suggesting? What sort of resistance might you be up against? The obvious way to do this is to speak to people, ask specific questions and then listen, carefully, and without becoming defensive. There's a lot to be said for the value you'll find in just listening. Using silence to give others the space to talk will often unearth a wealth of information which you'd never have found out through direct questioning. Also, make sure you're paying attention in meetings to comments or possible conflicts of interest. Consider all sides of your proposal and talk to whoever you need to beforehand to get the full picture before making a stand. Much better to be prepared for critics than be blind-sided.

Take responsibility for your own mindset

In one of Shakespeare's most famous plays, *Hamlet,* he wrote the line:

There is nothing either good or bad, but thinking makes it so.

This is a perfect summary of the concept that **we are the architects of our own reality.** If we believe that something is a certain way – sad, frustrating, energising, hopeful, our fault – then that is how it will be for us. This type of thinking dictates our reaction to a situation.

Undoubtedly, bad things will come our way – 'shit happens' as the saying goes – but it's our perception of that negative event which is key. We can choose to take control and spin the outcome in a positive way. In short, there is no situation so bad or so terrible that nothing good can be wrested from it.

Even in the heart-wrenching event of the death of a loved one, at some point after the initial shock and turmoil of emotions, you often hear people mention that they have found a new focus for life or that they have reassessed their lifestyle, or their priorities have now changed. There's even a term for it: post-traumatic growth (as used by mental-health expert Dr Olivia Remes).

Through a career and work lens, this way of thinking is important because you cannot control every situation that you end up in – but you **do** have the ability to take control of the story that you tell yourself about what has happened.

Let's look at an example. A team you've been working within has noticed that with some improvements to a number of internal processes, they could reduce duplicated tasks, lower costs and improve accuracy. As a team, you are due to present your findings at a board meeting at a different office the following week. You offered to lead the presentation and you've spent many hours practising. You're excited and nervous about the opportunity and can't wait to show everyone the improvement areas that you and the team have uncovered.

On the day of the presentation, you set off in your car early to get to the office in good time. A serious crash happens on the motorway a little way in front of you and the motorway is closed for recovery of the vehicles. You are stuck in stationary traffic.

After an hour, you realise that you're not going to make the meeting in time, even with the contingency you gave yourself, it's not going to be enough. You make the logical but hard decision to call your colleagues and tell them that someone else must lead the presentation. You will dial in and listen and get there as soon as you can.

You are gutted. You had seen this as your opportunity to shine in front of some very senior people and you were excited about the potential changes.

This can now go one of two ways; you can take the self-pitying route, telling yourself that this is so unfair, you were ready for this chance to prove yourself and now you've blown it. Walking in late to a board meeting, flustered and apologetic is not the way you wanted the directors to remember you. You'd feel defeated, low and frustrated. You'd probably carry that anger around with you all day and it would affect every other decision and conversation that you had. *'WHY DID THIS HAVE TO HAPPEN TO ME?'* you'd yell at the steering wheel.

The second route is taking responsibility for your story. The same facts are true, but you realise that there is absolutely nothing that you could have done to prevent the car crash, you had no control at all in missing the meeting. In fact, you're lucky not to be ten minutes earlier down the road and possibly involved in it. So – control the controllables. You accept that you won't be presenting the project and admit to yourself that your colleague is much more natural at presenting than you and will possibly get a better reaction to the requests for more resources.

As soon as you stop 'racing' in your head to get to the meeting and accept the situation for what it is, you free up your mind for more positive thoughts. The overall aim is to get approval for an ongoing project, so focus on how you can help in a more indirect way. You may not be at the centre of the presentation anymore, but you could still contribute, meaning that collectively you get the result you need and you support others to shine at the same time. There may also be other ways that you could still make a good impression on those at the meeting.

Staring at your fellow stuck motorway 'friends' you realise that this is perfect analogy for why you and the team want to change the processes that you've identified. The current system means that the individual actions (the cars) are too vulnerable to being affected by each other, forcing each other to slow down or stop entirely. The processes (lanes) aren't protected from each other and any small incident has a huge knock on effect for the whole system. After a quick call to your colleague, you agree that it would be a great illustration and a point of difference for your presentation to help the senior team to remember it.

Still in your car and parked up in the traffic jam you dial into the meeting and hear your colleague give a great summary of the project, in fact you pick up a few tips on things you could do to improve your presentation style. She then hands over to you and you use the camera on your phone to show the traffic jam that you're in and explain the impact that it has had on your morning. You make the connection with the business-critical systems which are currently vulnerable and overloaded and clearly demonstrate why the proposed improvements are so necessary.

The board is impressed and persuaded by the team's presentation and the plans to implement improvements are approved. You are delighted and feel that even given the circumstances, you pulled your weight and helped to get the nod to move forward. You've still been a key team member and together you've nailed it. The feelings following you around all day in this version of the scenario are undoubtedly more positive.

Taking responsibility for your own reality can revolutionise your thinking. When things have gone wrong or you've messed up, it's still important to reflect on how the situation unfolded, why things went awry and what you would change next time round to avoid it.

You're at the start of your river journey and it's only your first set of rapids. It's certain that there will be things you'll do differently next time you encounter some white water but keep things in perspective. The key is not to let negative thoughts overwhelm you. Try to talk yourself through it as you would talk to a friend: be honest, practical and kind.

ADAPT: PRIORITISE PROFESSIONAL DEVELOPMENT

After some rest and reflection, you rejoin the main current of the river feeling more confident, moving out of the lake on the other side. A large forest covers the left bank and blocks your view of anything on that side, but you can still see the river meandering ahead. In the distance the domed roofs of your palace are poking through the clouds, reminding you of its presence.

As you seem to be in a fairly easy portion of the river, you practice some new paddling and turning skills, having fun moving your body into different positions to affect the direction and balance of the boat. Your brain likes these smaller, non-life-threatening challenges and is fully engaged. After the last set of rapids, you now have some insight into the skills that the river will demand of you if you want to keep moving forward successfully, so you do what you can to prepare.

Quite happy and absorbed, you don't notice that the river ahead appears to vanish. What was more-or-less a straight channel suddenly takes an abrupt left-hand turn. Your brain slaps you around the face just in time and you swing the back of the boat around more than 90 degrees to adapt to this new course.

Having steadied the boat once again, you realise that the forest had been blocking your view of the continuing path of the river and there was no way you could have foreseen this change. Almost instantly your heart sinks as you realise that you're facing away from the palace. The reassuring glimpses you'd been having up until now are no longer there. A sense of loneliness, concern and nervousness now creeps into your body as you head ever forward, towards whatever now awaits you.

Feeling rested and prepared for the next event, you launch back into work with gusto. The first portion of the river has given you a taste of some of the challenges that you will encounter through your role. Your day-to-day tasks become more intuitive and you slowly start to find your feet. It's at this point that you'll probably start to notice where your knowledge or training gaps are appearing. Try to make time in your day to experiment with how you do things, explore new ideas and start reading. It's just like testing new paddling techniques in the boat while you have some calm water. In the quieter moments of your day, challenge yourself in small ways to see which things you can improve easily on your own and which may need some extra support.

This extra support doesn't have to be in the form of expensive courses. In our online life it would be impossible to not be aware of the abundance of sponsored posts for short, online training courses and adverts that follow you around on the internet as soon as you've done one search on 'management training'. As annoying as they can often be, they present a great opportunity to up-skill, get ahead of the competition or specialise.

Another option is to ask for or find a mentor or coach who could help you with certain skills or competencies. They can be internal or external to your organisation. No matter how you do it, the important point is to take it upon yourself to be constantly improving.

KEEP CHECKING IN WITH YOURSELF

In these first stages of your career journey, it's as much about adapting to the new external environment and the demands of the job as it is about adapting internally to the new emotions, pressures and triggers that will surface.

We're putting the foundations in place for a healthy and sustainable career, which means starting to develop new behaviours and habits that will put us on the right path over the long term. An important element of this is being conscious of what we're doing and how our body is reacting. Learning all sides of our uniqueness gives us strength and self-confidence.

This explains why we had a lie back in our boat after the first set of rapids. By watching the sky and running through how the challenge played out, we were reflecting and taking a step back to see things with a wider perspective. This slight distance and objectivity are perfect for learning. We notice the things we could have done differently and can plan ways to bring those changes into our next challenge.

On the river, we noticed how losing sight of our palace made us feel nervous and concerned. By recognising those reactions, we can find ways to seek reassurance again and re-set the balance. You could try a visualisation exercise of you living a day in the future in your 'goal' world or doing some brainstorming of what your goal looks, feels, sounds and even smells like. Help to reassure your brain and your heart that you're still focused and not about to let the boat drift.

The rapids in the previous stage of your journey also opened your eyes to the physical and mental strain that you can come under in the intense phases of delivering an important project or task. The break on the lake was very restorative and you have bounced back quickly, but don't miss the lesson here: **your health and wellbeing are your own responsibility.** This is as much about setting up healthy habits for the long term as it is about what you need right now.

When you are young you feel that you can go forever and run on empty. That is true for a while, but if you don't start to integrate positive habits into your life now, then you'll find yourself in burn-out territory by the time you're 40 – just at the point where you imagined yourself taking on the really serious, senior roles that you've been dreaming about.

Everyone is physically capable of feeling stress. The difference comes in how we process that stress and react to it. According to medical bodies, two of the key elements to managing stress well are those we have already covered:

1. **Stop and rest.** Give yourself a mental and physical break to allow for recuperation and reflection.

2. **Take control:** An optimistic attitude and an ability to unearth a positive within a bad situation will mean that you don't end up

wallowing in self-pity and getting into a negative downward spiral of trash-talking yourself. While it is important to acknowledge the negative emotions and spend time working through the underlying issues; letting this become your only focus is not healthy.

Along, successful and sustainable career needs energy, focus and awareness, all of which require a fit and healthy body. While the occasional 'unhealthy' behaviour is totally normal and won't have any real long-term impact, unhealthy habits can often come back to bite you in the end, so my advice is to aim for overall good health and you'll never be sorry.

The foundations of good health are very easy and are based on 4 core factors:

★ **Breathing:** As much as it is an automatic function of our bodies, it also has enormous power to calm, connect, restore and focus our bodies. There are many breathing techniques which can be used, from 1-minute calming deep-breathing to longer, transformational breathing practises to completely relax and reset our whole body. Understanding how to use your breath to control your emotions and reactions can be game-changing when it comes to stressful work situations. Instead of letting a person or a situation dictate how you feel, you can use your breath to put you back in the driving seat.

★ **Sleeping:** Don't underestimate it or treat it lightly. Your body uses sleep time for essential repair and processing activities. Your brain can't function properly without sleep, your digestive system can't process our food efficiently and your emotional barometer is affected. It doesn't have to be eight hours every night – we are all different. Find out what sleep pattern works best for you and then keep it consistent eighty per cent of the time. You won't regret it.

★ **Moving:** Moving doesn't have to be strenuous exercise, it can be just what it sounds like: getting your body out of one position and into another. Moving yourself away from a screen, standing up, looking out of a window and rolling your shoulders wakes your muscles up, resets your eyes on a different point of focus, gets your blood moving to detoxify your system and allows your brain to rest. Getting into nature – or absorbing nature – at regular intervals during the day has been proven to have an exponentially beneficial effect on our entire mental and physical well-being. So go for that lunchtime walk and stand up to look out of the window next time you make a call.

★ **Feeling:** The ability to consciously notice what triggers your emotions is an incredibly powerful tool to be able to call on. It allows you to optimise your life to get the best out of it because you can focus on what makes you feel content and energised. You can manage challenging emotions with patience and empathy and you can connect with others.

Start prioritising your health and wellbeing straightaway and your career will benefit. You'll have as much energy and enthusiasm in twenty years' time as you do now!

We've now come to a pause in our river journey. The ADAPT phase is complete and we'll soon be moving into the more challenging GROW stage. Before we leave this first portion, it may be useful to cover some practical tips on how to manage the situations that we've encountered so far. These tips are drawn from my practical experiences and bring out the main things I wished I could have told myself in the early part of my career.

ADAPT: EXERCISE 4

Put yourself in the best possible position by considering your own needs and preferences in advance. It's much easier to refer to a list that you've already got to hand when you're busy or stressed, than trying to think of things 'on the fly'.

★ How do you best relax and how you best de-stress? They can be different things. For example, if I want to relax I might do some yoga or read a fiction book, but if I need to de-stress then I know that I need something active and energetic, so I might go for a walk or a run or go to the gym. Write a few options down which will account for different weather conditions, a variety of locations, a mix of long and short activities, who you might be with, the space/surroundings you may have, etc. The aim is to get to a list which you can refer to any time you need a bit of headspace and you can choose something that will hit the spot.

★ Look at the digital options. There are lots of great apps and tools around for mindfulness and meditation aimed at all levels. You can find guided talks, meditations, music, drawing, all with the aim of helping to re-set your busy mind. And many are free ... so no excuses!

★ We have looked at the importance recognising the need for continued personal development, so how do you best like to learn? What job-specific knowledge gaps and soft skills would you like to improve?

ADAPT: PRACTICAL TIPS

EXPLORE YOUR TRAINING AND DEVELOPMENT OPTIONS

Everything we have covered in the ADAPT phase focuses on building our awareness of where we are now and where we want to go. By highlighting the gaps between these two points we can build a plan of action to keep us moving forward with intent. This is where training and development become your friend. Learning new things opens us up to new opportunities. New opportunities mean change. Change means progress. Progress feels positive and rewarding. So make sure continued training and development are a permanent part of your career plan.

Every company has a hugely different idea as to what constitutes training and development. Quality and availability can vary year on year and even between departments. It's also often out of date in terms of up-to-the-minute technology. Let's be honest, your business probably isn't a training specialist and as such you can't rely on it to fulfil your every training need. As a general rule, I would advise that you use internal training for information on processes and policies within the business and look externally for your personal development training.

You can Google training on X, Y and Z as well as the next person, so instead of labouring the point of HOW to find training, I just want to stress that you should go to credible and reliable sources. Organisations like Linked In Learning, Google Academy and the various Chartered Institutes for the industry area are great places to start. TED talks are also fantastic for inspiration and new ways to think, and they cover just about any topic you could bring to mind.

The point is – take responsibility for your own learning. Spot your gaps and fill them. Try to prioritise content which is in your preferred learning style; do you need to see example videos, do you prefer to read information, can you absorb things better by listening or do you need to do it yourself and learn as you go? It makes a big difference to how well you retain the training.

If you're not sure about your learning style, then you could work through a learning-styles questionnaire to get a sense of how best you take in new information. The famous one by Honey and Mumford is very well-regarded and is based on the acclaimed David Kolb's learning cycle theory. It takes you through questions to reveal whether you are an Activist, Pragmatist, Theorist or Reflector. It explores your learning style by looking at your preference when approaching a new task: do you prefer concrete experience or observation or active experimentation or abstract thinking? It takes into account your preferred physical AND emotional response. Honey and Mumford say that everyone has preference for one – in some cases two – style(s) of learning, which then dictate(s) when you learn best, when you are least likely to learn and which activities are the most suitable for you to optimise your learning. More information and links are in the further reading section at the end of the book.

It's also important to have some fun with your learning. Alongside the more serious, dry training, try to find some lighter, more enjoyable topics which can help you at work, such as creative writing, logic puzzles or business games. These can help your brain get used to idea generation and lateral thinking, which is when you approach a problem from a different perspective to try to see a new solution. These often don't come naturally unless you practise, meaning that you may be the only person in a team to have these skills at your disposal. This can be very useful at work when a fresh approach or creative problem-solving is required and you can demonstrate a unique point of view.

MAKE HABITS WORK FOR YOU

Once you have thought about your goal career persona, habits are a key way to help you unlock your potential and increase your chances of getting there.

Habits are simply learnt and reinforced behaviours that we have done so often that our conscious brain doesn't need to think about the act of doing them anymore; our subconscious has taken over and we do them automatically.

Habits are triggered by a cue-craving-response-reward pattern that Charles Duhigg explored in his book *The Power of Habit*. This is a loop whereby our body recognises a cue (a smell, a time of day, a feeling) and then that triggers a craving for something. We then do something to satisfy our craving, this action then produces a positive feeling that we take as a reward and it reinforces our initial behaviour to the cue. This works even for habits that we know are 'bad', the knowledge of it being bad for us doesn't override the positive reward we get from satisfying our craving.

We know that our actions (and therefore our habits) speak volumes about the type of person we are, so it follows that if we want to develop into the type of person that we identified in our Palace goal, then we have to look at how we act.

It's an interesting exercise to go through a couple of days and try to consciously notice what your habits are. This is easier said than done as it is our subconscious at the helm, but with some effort you can do it. Let's have a look at a work-day example: what is your meeting routine? How much do you think about how you prepare for and act within a meeting?

Let's take a reoccurring, ordinary meeting and use the loop described above. The meeting reminder in your calendar goes off 15 mins before the meeting. This is your **cue** for your body to **crave** a little more time to get your current task finished, so you are triggered into a **response** to hit the *'snooze until 5 minutes before'* action on the reminder and you get the **reward** that the reminder disappears to give you ten more minutes to finish your task. The issue with this habit becomes apparent ten minutes later. When the reminder goes off this time, you still haven't quite finished your task, but you now only have five minutes before your meeting. In this five minutes, you wanted a toilet break before you start AND to get a fresh cup of coffee AND you wanted to look over the minutes of the last meeting to jog your memory of the topics for discussion this time around. Five minutes isn't enough time to do all of this so you either arrive to the meeting late or/and underprepared.

My guess is that late, underprepared and stressed aren't behaviours that you'd imagined when you created your future job persona. Someone doing your future role would be early to a meeting, as this would give them chance to talk to people beforehand and perhaps pick up some useful information as well as build relationships. This person would be prepared with some useful and thought-provoking questions to debate. Finally, this person would be calm and open, in a perfect state to debate a point of difference or make a rational argument for their opinion without getting flustered or irritated. You are fully capable of all of these behaviours but you're not giving yourself the best chance at demonstrating this side of yourself, all because of the negative habit hitting the snooze button on the meeting reminder. So this is a habit that needs changing.

The best way to change a habit is to look at the system which created the habit and try to change that. Look at the cues and the reasons that you do something and then eliminate them or do something differently.

Let's go back to our meeting example. You realise

that the short-term belief that you can finish a task in ten minutes is over-riding your longer-term goal of giving yourself the best opportunity to shine in a meeting. If you're honest with yourself, it is, in fact, rare that you complete that piece of work in the ten minutes you have left and to your normal high standard. Usually it's either rushed, so needs re-doing or not completed at all, so needs more time dedicating to it after the meeting.

Realising that this belief is driving your behaviour means you can change it. You are currently using the system (the meeting reminder) to trigger and reinforce your habit, but what if you used it to trigger different response instead? This type of thinking is a classic case of taking responsibility for your actions.

The change needed to the system which supports your current habit is actually quite simple: When the meeting reminder pings onto your screen **(cue)**, instead of 'snoozing' it, you treat it as a gift because it has just given you fifteen minutes to practise behaviours that will take you closer to your goal career persona **(craving)**. You get up out of your chair, which signals to your body that you're shifting activity and your brain start to move away from your previous task, getting ready for the next one **(response)**. You go to the toilet and get your fresh drink. You then arrive at the meeting early and take the time to read through the previous minutes, making notes on the issues to be raised. By the time others arrive, you feel ready, 'in the moment' and calm **(reward)**. All because you changed a habit of snoozing a reminder.

Once you have done this a couple of times and your

body realises that it gets a bigger reward from the new behaviour than it did from the old one, it will start to prompt you to do the new action instead ... and so your new habit is born.

By thinking of the person that you want to become, you can associate the habits that this future 'you' would have with where you are now. By finding the gaps or changes that you want to make, every change in habit is one step closer to your goal ... and the best part is that by following this method you feel like you are gaining something by changing a habit and not losing something.

Think of a habit that you'd like to change or adopt. What could be a first step in creating a new response to a particular cue?

If you'd like to learn more about the methods and science behind habit change then take a look at James Clear's work.

GET PLUGGED IN

Plug yourself into the internal communications channels and digital networks around the business which will keep you up to date on useful information such as:

★ Central business strategy and progress

★ Big contract/new business wins

★ Important clients/customer segments

★ Effects of market trends

★ Your department's strategy and progress

★ Which departments or programmes get the biggest teams and the largest budgets (this shows you where the focus of the business is and can be very useful)

I've had many occasions in the past when I have bumped into the CEO or the MD in the office and knowing about the business performance and current news meant that I felt confident enough to speak to them and engage in a little small talk, rather than feeling intimidated and saying a quiet 'hello' while opening the latest ping on my phone. It can be worthwhile thinking of a short question that you can have at your fingertips for such occasions, such as, *"Have you noticed that the situation in XX or with XX is having any direct impact on the business?"* or, *"It was interesting to see XX happen last week, is the new strategic focus on XX intended to support this?"* In my case, it may not have made any impression on them at all, but it gave me a huge boost to feel that I had held my own and shown them that I was engaged and eloquent on company matters.

FIND YOUR SUBJECT MATTER EXPERTS (SMEs)

SMEs will be all over the business and can cover anything from sustainability to operational process to IT system development. Having access to the SMEs most relevant for your area of work can be invaluable as they are a short-cut to the information that you need to know AND how it's relevant to your business. Make sure the relationship is reciprocal and offer your help and advice whenever you can to help cement these SMEs in your close circle of colleagues.

This is more relevant in a larger business, where thousands of people will all have their own specialisms. In smaller businesses, though, this is still important, but it may just mean getting to know your smaller team of colleagues much better. Perhaps someone in finance has a side-hustle in website-building or your HR Manager has an interest in graphic design. You'll never know until you start talking to them.

My brain is much happier in a creative and language-orientated task than it is with numbers and data, but my roles leading complex, international digital marketing and systems projects have demanded an equal focus on all these elements. This is where my SMEs come in. I asked for one-to-one meetings with a Finance Manager, an IT Systems Developer, a Website Coder and a Business Analyst. I was very open about my weakness in these areas and very specific about what I wanted them to help me with.

I just took each task one step at a time, making sure I was learning and implementing as much as possible myself so that I was making good use of their time. I made lots of notes and with practice I learnt to talk comfortably about these topics to a certain level of detail – and crucially, I could recognise the point at which I needed to hand over to an expert.

Over time I became more and more expert in each area and, although my brain still winces every time I need to tackle data analysis or a budget reconciliation, it has become easier. I've now got great relationships with these SMEs and our mutual recognition of each other's strengths and areas for support means we are supportive and encouraging of each other, willing to help whenever we can.

BE COLLABORATIVE

In the early stages of your career (and of any new project) you need to hear from everyone who has an opinion on the work you are doing or is affected by it. These stakeholders will influence the success of your project, so make sure you understand everyone's views and have addressed them to a greater or lesser extent. Yes, it will be time-consuming. Yes, it will get repetitive and annoying. Yes, you will have to speak to people who you don't particularly like and yes, you will have to just sit and take it when someone says something that you wholly disagree with (this isn't the time to take them on). You still have to do it!

You will learn very quickly which views carry the most weight and have the biggest impact and don't be tempted to dismiss the negative voices. Talk to as many people as possible, mention your work in as many meetings as you can to weed out any opinions that you may have missed and focus on just listening in a collaborative way.

One of my favourite sayings (from Greek philosopher, Epictetus) is very relevant here: 'We have two ears and one mouth so that we can listen twice as much as we speak.' You are not working in a silo and if a piece of work that you're doing doesn't impact anyone else, then I would question why you are doing it in the first place. Always go into the BIG meeting or presentation with as many opinions and reservations as possible already accounted for. This will mean the decision-making is much more straightforward and hopefully less of a surprise to anyone in the room.

I learnt the hard way that collaboration is critical. On a number of occasions, I didn't ask the right questions or listen closely enough to project stakeholders before important meetings and it led to frustration, delays and embarrassment. I can now see that had I been more collaborative and communicative with the decision-makers individually BEFORE the meeting, I could have worked through the concerns and demonstrated the individual benefits in more personal setting. This in turn would have meant using the meeting purely as a collective stamp of approval, rather than a discussion forum. Everyone would all have left the meeting feeling confident in the decision, pleased with the progress and reassured that all members were on board. Instead, the confused debate that ensued left negative feelings, frustration, lost time and huge stress on my side while I tried to reverse the decision.

LEARN THE JARGON

I swear that most businesses have more TLAs (three-letter acronyms) than the world has languages. A company's unique jargon can be multilayered and impenetrable ... and you will need to be fluent in it! To be taken seriously in a business you need to understand and be able to use the appropriate jargon and acronyms. Of course, you will come across ones you don't know and in those cases, always ask rather than pretend, but the most commonly used terms should become natural to you very quickly.

If you're not confident to ask for a meaning within the meeting, then the next time you come across a bizarre TLA, just open up a blank email or word doc and make a note of it. You can then take your list to someone you trust – your boss or friendly colleague – and ask if they can help you work them out. It shows initiative, enables you to grow and builds honest relationships they will appreciate.

BUILD A SUPPORT NETWORK

As we saw in the river journey, your work will be intense, stressful and all-consuming at times and you'll need support. You should always have the support of your line management, but I'm talking more about the people who you go to when you need to complain, shout, cry or just need a laugh and a distraction.

Having a network within your business is just as important as your close friends and family. Your work 'family' understands your job and your day-to-day life better than those outside, so they will be able to help, listen and sympathise in way that no one else can. Try to find support in different offices/ teams and at different levels within the business too. The wider and more varied your network, the more useful and supportive it can be. Don't be afraid to reach out to colleagues for help and advice; the worst they can say is no, then you just leave them to it and find someone else!

I'm sure you're smart enough to figure out ways to do this which feel right for you, but some ideas that I've seen work in the past are where people have got together to:

★ Go for a run or walk either at lunchtime or after work in the area around the office

★ Create an inter-departmental baking competition

★ Do a team charity event

★ Create a book club

★ Take part in a fantasy sports league

Some people will always hate manufactured 'get togethers', but if you're someone who enjoys meeting new people and getting involved, then it's worth a shot.

Understanding your colleagues better also builds on the theme of empathy because the enjoyment of your job is going to affected by the mood and reactions of those around you. We all know that the best friendships are two-way and this is just as true with your colleagues. Several times I've taken colleagues on an enforced 'walk' outside as I've noticed their stress and anxiety levels rising, but they don't feel that they can say anything in an open office. Taking the initiative and approaching them rather than waiting for them to ask for help is often the quickest way to nip an issue in the bud, helping them to get some perspective or just providing a friendly ear to let them get it out of their system.

FIND YOUR CHEERLEADERS

You are ambitious and driven but you can't get to the palace on your own. Cheerleaders are people in the business who will champion you and your work, even when you're not in the room.

Cheerleaders are usually the most effective when

they are senior to you and operating in slightly different circles.

The aim is to demonstrate to them your whole breadth of skills, experiences and knowledge, so when something relevant comes up and you're not present, these people will consider you – either to pass information on, volunteer that someone speak to you or suggest you for an activity. Let them know what you're doing and your successes, also new ideas or solutions to problems you have noticed.

These people need a little extra attention from you. Is there anything extra that you can give to a joint project or area of interest? Could you help them with anything additional? Engage with them on your professional interests and share new ideas. You essentially want to show them the best you can be.

As before, be receptive to colleagues coming to you for similar support, pay it forward and you never know when your rewards will come or in what form they will take.

HAVE MORE THAN ONE GOAL

We've talked about the palace being your ultimate goal, but it is also important to have short and medium-term goals to keep you focused and give you a way to mark your progress. It's much easier to ignore the distraction of new streams splitting off from your river if your next check point is within reach. Take responsibility of mapping out a few realistic and exciting milestones which can help keep you on the right path and also keep your interest and energy levels up.

If your palace or goal persona is the Director

of Innovation and Technology, then perhaps your milestones may be to lead a small innovation project within your department. Put yourself forward to trial a new technology or create a working group across different functions whose aim is to suggest and support innovation within their remit. Make active and purposeful steps towards these goals and let people know what you want and why.

Finally, acknowledge and celebrate the wins! It's critical to recognise a milestone and acknowledge it as a win. Wins make us feel good, show that we're contributing, build on our confidence, demonstrate our progress and give us something to talk to colleagues about – so make sure you know when they happen! Have a go-to list of treats, small and big ones, which you can indulge in when it's time for a celebration. By taking the time to congratulate yourself, you're reflecting on the effort it took to get there and you're rewarding that hard work, which sets you up to repeat that behaviour in the future. It's also fun and gives you a mental lift – so crack open the box of luxury chocolates and enjoy!

START A JOURNAL

This can be in any form you like: audio notes, videos, free writing, daily diary etc. We touched on the importance of reflection and self-understanding when we were at the lake after the first set of rapids. This is the mechanism to do that.

The initial reaction to this idea is often, *'I don't have time, I don't see the point, it's just not me,'* but I would argue that this is one of the most powerful self-improvement techniques you can do, so try to park your reservations until you've tried it.

I find that there is something very therapeutic and satisfying about getting the swirling thoughts and feelings which are racing around my head down onto paper or in some external form. Once on paper, they lose their power and I can assess them much more rationally and impartially. I can spot patterns, see assumptions and notice how crazy some of the stuff in my head is – even when it seems perfectly logical within the confines of my brain!

Try to journal on your good days and your bad ones; notice whom you spoke to, what you did, what triggers made you feel a certain way, which outcomes were good and which ones were bad, and what would you do differently. There's no judgment here and this isn't intended as a stick to bash yourself with; it's simply a way to notice that you could do something differently next time.

Try it for a month before you disregard it – trust me, it makes a difference!

We're ready to move on now and carry on with our journey. Back at the river, the next stage of our journey is going to test us in new ways. We can never know what is around the next corner, so let's head into it prepared, alert and excited by the opportunities. Let's GROW!

GROW

- LOOK FOR IMPROVEMENTS

After the shock of the abrupt turn in the river, you realise that you have a stretch of fairly calm water ahead for a short distance. Knowing that this can be short-lived and the uncertainty around when you may get another break, you take full advantage. Your brain and your heart kick-back, letting thoughts and emotions bubble through you at their own pace.

Letting the boat move slowly forward with the current, you reflect, your brain and heart both giving their input: Your skills at dealing with the rapids have improved and you remember that they can even be enjoyable, re-living the thrill and adrenaline. But your brain reminds you that they were relatively small ones last time, so you can't get complacent.

You get a sudden flash of inspiration. You'd forgotten that you'd almost lost your oar a couple of times in the last set of rapids and now that you have some quiet time, you could figure out a way to attach it to the boat so that you don't have to worry about that happening in future. You've still not got much with you, but your eye caught sight of an old piece of fishing line that was trailing along behind you, seemingly caught on the side of the boat. It wasn't perfect but it would certainly give you some security and a few extra seconds to react if the next set of rapids decided to take a swipe at your oar. After a couple of minutes fiddling with the line, you find a way to secure it to the boat and the oar in a way that still gives you freedom to move. Job done!

You sit down again and consider the disappointment you felt when you realised your palace was no longer in view and your heart does a little sad sigh. Yes, it's true that you can't directly see it anymore, but it hasn't gone anywhere and actually if you close your eyes it appears instantly in your mind's eye, large, beautiful and alluring. So, you make a conscious choice to move on from that thought and instead focus on the exciting possibilities that lie ahead. What's next?!

The GROW phase of your career is all about consolidating what you know, facing new challenges and building your resilience. I call it 'The Messy Middle' because you'll find yourself being pulled in different directions and questioning yourself one week and then having some wonderful experiences and enjoying every minute the next!

Just as in this last part of the story, getting into good habits around reflecting and learning can reap tangible rewards. In this case, your thinking time led to a realisation that you could improve the boat to help you in the future. In real life, this translates to you building on a skill or equipping yourself with something which will mean that you're more resilient when the next challenge presents itself.

During the ADAPT phase of our journey, we looked at how our three Guiding Principles provided a good foundation to understanding the new world around you. Now that you're entering the GROW phase, let's look at how they apply when we're facing new challenges.

Take Responsibility

At this point in your career, taking responsibility means learning to assess your options quickly by calculating risks and applying your knowledge to that which is in front of you. It means using your experience to apply a 'best guess' and then making a decision, knowing you've got the skills to face what's coming without getting paralysed by indecision. No one has all the answers, but we all have a lot to contribute so get yourself into a position where you can be brave and trust yourself. Starting in a new career gives you the option to do things differently: disrupting, pushing boundaries and going outside of your comfort zone, so we'll be looking at HOW you can do these things in a confident way.

It's important to take responsibility for your own attitude too. The Messy Middle is just that, messy, so there will be times when it feels tough, frustrating, stressful, pointless and boring. With your goal seemingly further away than ever it is a prime time to want to change course completely to a safe, calm, predictable route (as we'll see in the next installment of our river story). My guess, however, is that you'd fairly quickly drift into boredom and listlessness down this path, no matter how appealing it seems at the time.

It's also worth considering that when something appears to be easy, you can be certain that it will hold its own set of challenges, even if that challenge is how to reverse out of it when you get stuck! So, we'll think about how to avoid getting taken down this path.

We touched on the importance of noticing our feelings during ADAPT, as one of the cornerstones of good health alongside sleep, breathing and movement. Only you can notice your feelings and instead of being swept away by them, it's important to try to accept them for what they are and realise that no feelings are forever. The very nature of feelings is that they are all short-term and reactive. So give yourself some time or try to turn them around and see if there is another side to them. You are in control of your feelings, not the other way around. You can manage them, explore them and change them with practice. We'll spend some time on the Wheel of Perspective which is a great tool to use when you're feeling overwhelmed to help you come back to a more balanced place.

Taking responsibility for your attitude and reactions to situations will determine how they impact you, what you gain from them and how others view you. It will also dictate how much fun you have along the way. Learning to enjoy the ride is half the battle! Don't wait for time to have fun, find fun in what you're doing, otherwise you could find you're spending all your timing waiting.

We'll also explore the importance of taking a wide view: looking left and right as well as straight ahead and not looking back with regret. Your career is always moving forward. Going back is incredibly hard work, a waste of energy and, more often than not, disappointing.

Show Empathy

Your empathy skills are always on call at every stage of your career, but you'll notice that as you progress deeper into the journey, they take on a new significance and usefulness. As you start taking bold decisions and challenging the *status quo* you'll naturally be raising your head above the parapet and becoming more visible. This brings with it many positives, but you will also notice that the number of people who disagree with you seems to increase. This isn't your judgement taking a nosedive, but just that you are appearing on the radar of more and more people, so naturally you'll see more opinions. In this section, we'll consider how this can appear in a work scenario and how to use empathy to get comfortable with disagreement. Shortly we'll be doing our Deep Dive into this second principle so that we can really understand its significance.

Know Yourself

This principle is going to be more important than ever in this phase of your career. You'll get tested in many ways and from different sides, so having the strong support structure and positive habits in place from the ADAPT phase will help you develop the resilience you'll need. We'll discuss some of the scenarios which often crop up at this point and work through how to listen to your gut, which will enable you to be brave and take the important decisions, whilst also protecting yourself.

GUIDING PRINCIPLES DEEP DIVE 2: SHOW EMPATHY

We all think we have empathy but putting it into practise can be a different matter entirely. It's the eternal battle between the selfish need to satisfy ourselves and the wisdom that we are better humans when we collaborate, listen and seek the views of others. It's especially important in the GROW phase of our career journey because we will be at the point where our decisions and actions are starting to have an impact on people. By using empathy, we can ensure that our decisions are well-informed and founded in solid reasoning. As we test new skills and push our comfort zones in this phase, we'll also need the support and understanding of those around us, not least because it's likely that we'll get some things wrong and we need these solid relationships to help us fail and learn in a safe place.

It can be seen in a negative light, as a soft skill or a feminine trait, but the simple fact is that every person will respond better to someone who engages with them in a positive way. That doesn't mean simply agreeing with someone or giving them what they want, it means being respectful, considerate, open and honest.

Luckily the tide appears to be turning in the public perception of empathy as a core leadership skill. Traditionally, it used to be seen as a weakness, but some very successful and famous leaders across all sectors are now calling it out as an essential component.

So how do you learn, use and show empathy? There are two important elements which are worth spending some time on:

Planning for the long-term is traditionally a

mindset that comes with age and experience, but if you can adopt it at this point in your journey, early in your career, it will pay you back ten-fold. Once you have a goal clear in your mind, it may seem logical to try to get there in the most direct way possible, focusing all your actions and energies on ensuring that you are pushing yourself forward as fast as possible.

However, as I mentioned before, there's little chance that you will achieve this goal on your own. If it's a senior position that you are looking to hold, there is no value in getting there and then realising that no one in the team around you respects or values you. Your 'power' will be minimal and your impact fleeting. A much smarter plan is to play the long game and use the time to build the team and network you'll need later.

With this in mind, in the short term try looking around you to see who else you can support. Just as your career path is uncertain, so is everyone's and by helping your colleagues to rise up, you'll all benefit. Use empathy and intuition to build bridges at every opportunity and help out your colleagues whenever you can. Collective support and achievement undoubtedly feel more rewarding than a solitary rise to lonely fame.

All our negative emotions and reactions come from fear. Perhaps it's the fear of the unknown, the fear of change, the fear of looking stupid or the fear of failing but I only discovered later in my career that they can all lead to negativity. You would never expose your innermost fears to your colleagues, and neither would they in return – but it's guaranteed that you both have them. In this case, empathy is learning to temper your reaction to an event or a conversation with the thought, *'Perhaps there's something going on for this person that I don't understand and that is why they reacted as they did.'*

I will warn you that this is much easier said than done, but with practice it can become more instinctive. The selfish child inside us all would make every situation about us and I have certainly been there! Early on in my career I was a marketing executive and the only person dedicated to marketing within the organisation. I worked very closely with my manager and although he was much more experienced than me in most areas, he didn't have much marketing knowledge; he tended to give me ultimate responsibility and authority over the marketing activity. This was a wonderful learning experience and I was certainly dropped in the deep end on many occasions, but overall I flourished in this style of relationship.

In hindsight, it also led me to a level of confidence and arrogance about my position in the company. On one occasion, my manager was presenting to an influential group of senior directors and investors and he'd asked me to attend. I believed that I was there to add value and that my attendance was a reflection of my position, however I now realise that he actually thought it would be a good learning experience for me (so we were already at cross-purposes).

I was so wrapped up in the idea of my status at this important meeting that it didn't occur to me wonder how my manager may be feeling about his presentation. He was nervous and I'd missed it. When he realised that he was short of some photocopies he needed just as the meeting was about to start, he asked me to do them for him (and miss the start of the meeting) in a very direct and blunt manner. I met the request with a very resentful and clearly unhappy, 'Fine'. When I came back into the room with the photocopies while the meeting was in full swing, I made it clear from my body language that I felt that I shouldn't have had to do them.

At the end of the meeting, I was still holding onto a feeling that I'd been wronged in some way. He spoke to me afterwards and queried my attitude. He explained that there had been a lot riding on his presentation and he'd been hoping for my support to help him out in his last-minute panic when he had realised he didn't have the documents he needed.

Needless to say, I felt shame flood through me. I had been so consumed by my own (insignificant) presence in the meeting and my own reputation that I'd missed a colleague who needed my help in a stressful moment. Empathy would have given me a different perspective and changed my emotional response. He would have felt grateful (rather than confused and angry) and I would have moved past the request quickly and taken in the experience of the meeting (rather than stewing over some imagined slight). Lesson learnt!

GROW: TAP INTO YOUR SUBCONSCIOUS

As in the ADAPT portion of the journey, the priority

here is allowing yourself reflection and relaxation or downtime. This is for two main reasons.

The first is that it doesn't happen very often, so take it when it arrives. Professional life for an ambitious and motivated person can be seriously demanding of your time and energy so burn-out and stress are very easy dead-ends to head into. We'll look into some of the possible pitfalls of professional life in the THRIVE section, but they're worth a mention here too. The secret to avoiding them is all based on awareness, knowing yourself and taking responsibility. You need to be able to recognise in yourself the signs of overwhelm at an early stage, understand your options and then take whatever positive action is needed to head it off and right yourself again. It's important that you do all three of these – it's no good spotting that you're overworked but then assuming nothing can change and ploughing on regardless.

The second reason is that by pausing and reflecting, you're giving your brain some time to fill you in on all the subconscious work it has been doing. Your subconscious is like the quiet, shy, super-intelligent child in a class who sits patiently with her hand up, waiting to be asked to share what she knows. So, while the rest of your body may make itself know loudly, by aches, pains or constant chatter, your subconscious is quietly busy. She is processing all the information, images and feelings that have happened recently. She's making links, creating new thoughts and referring back to past information. This is where your imagination solves problems, offers new ideas, invents entirely new concepts and generally makes you look awesome!

However, unless you give her some quiet space and the focused respect she deserves, your subconscious will keep all of this gold to herself. We saw this in the story when you realised that you should be looking to secure the oar to the boat, but let me give you a real-life example of this in action.

As part of one of my roles, I was flying frequently between Ireland and the UK. This is only a very short flights, but nevertheless, I would usually be responding to emails or working on a presentation. On one occasion I'd been at a marketing meeting all day in Dublin, talking about brand strategies for how to organise the many smaller brands we had sitting under the main brand and how to promote a new brand that was going live in the near future. It had been an intense day, considering and debating lots of opinions, facts and examples. We had made good progress but hadn't really nailed down the best way to manage the new brand.

My head was buzzing by the time I was on the flight, but I was tired, so instead of pulling out my laptop I sat back and closed my eyes, letting my attention drift. About halfway through the 35-minute flight I suddenly had a flash of inspiration. My subconscious had my attention. It reminded me of some comments that a colleague had made weeks earlier, alongside a brand identity strategy that I'd noticed on a website the day before while doing some research. Combining these elements with some of the challenges that we'd talked through that day at the meeting and I could suddenly see a solution. It could work!

I stayed with my eyes closed while I considered the idea more closely from all angles. By the time we landed I was sure it was a good idea. Sitting in my car in the airport multi-storey car park half an hour later, I wrote a draft email with all the details in it and saved it for the following day.

The next morning in the office I read it back and confirmed to myself that it wasn't a crazy figment of my tired imagination but a solid idea that had real potential. I sent it around to the team. The praise and excitement that I got back was confirmation in itself. After that I never worked on those short flights, Instead, I sat down with my eyes closed and asked my subconscious, "So what have you got for me today?"

GROW: EXERCISE 1

In order to GROW, we need to learn how to switch off from all the external noise and take note of our internal compass:

★ When was the last time you just day-dreamed or just chilled out with no distractions – no phones, music, people or pings demanding your attention? Why not try some downtime without any sounds at all, just focusing on the natural sounds around you and tuning in to how you feel.

★ If you're finding it hard to slow down your brain, try to focus on just one thing: perhaps some lyrics to the last song you heard or a piece of dialogue in your favourite film or your favourite sporting moment of the last year. Don't get distracted by other thoughts, just give a virtual nod in their direction and tell them you'll be back to them later; for now, it's just you and your one-focus thought.

★ Give your conscious brain something to do while you

let your subconscious have the space it needs; try the #mindfulminute videos on the @findyourwingsuk Instagram and Facebook feeds. These one-minute videos of a calming scene in nature will let you watch something while not making you 'think'.

★ Think of the problem you're trying to solve and start writing about it. Words. Sentences. Expletives(!). Whatever comes to mind. Free flow and don't try to make sense of it, just put down whatever comes into your mind. You might be surprised by the little nuggets that you uncover.

GROW: ASSESS ALL CHOICES

Breaking out of your reverie, you snap to attention as you realise that in front of you, the river splits into three. What's going on here?! You brain leaps into action, trying to find a solution. Two of the bigger channels follow roughly the same direction and have what look like the early signs of rapids just at the edge of your sight range. The third, smaller route winds around slowly, taking a lazy route almost back the way you've come… which could be a more direct route to your palace … or it could dry up into an unnavigable puddle!

You weigh up each option, finding as much information as you can on their speed, depth, width and length. There is so much unknown with them all, you can feel panic start to rise in your chest. The larger two look pretty terrifying, but your heart reminds you that you enjoyed the thrill of the rapids last time … and you've been practising! The smaller route, however appealing its calm, easy waters seem at first glance, could end up giving you more headaches. You notice that even your brain isn't leaping at the idea of an easier ride on this third channel; the potential downsides of getting stuck and having to force your way back against the current are a serious consideration. With these best guesses and knowing your own confidence and skills, you make a decision on one of the channels, just moments before your boat is swept into the bank. *'Phew! About time!'* your brain shrieks at you, *'What more were you waiting for? An invitation?!'*

You chose the first channel. It thanks you by throwing you almost immediately into the biggest rapids you've experienced so far. *'Wrong decision!'* your brain taunts you, but your heart is joyous. *'This is what I'm talking about, I love this stuff!!'* it cries.

It takes all of your strength, balance and concentration to keep afloat. You're knocked down three or four times by the force of the water and partially submerged rocks but you persevere. The deep growl of excitement and the push of the adrenaline give you the extra strength you need.

As the rapids flatten out, you anticipate a break. This is not to be, as a stretch of tricky bends come into view. Your brain is not impressed. *'Didn't we taunt death enough with that last stretch? This is really asking for trouble.'* You heart quietens the Drama Queen: *'It doesn't look so bad. We can do this!'*

After the rapids, these bends in the river feel like a walk in the park and you're now strong and confident enough to navigate your boat successfully. You've smashed it! You're grinning broadly.

Your brain doesn't leave you to celebrate for too long though – it starts to wonder what the other routes would have been like. *'Would they have been shorter? Would they have got you to your palace quicker? Would the rapids have been gentler?"*

Maybe, but also they may have been longer with new, more challenging difficulties. You'll never know. In fact, it is irrelevant as you made a choice, dealt with whatever was in front of you and made the best of the present moment. Now you have to live with the consequences. You remind yourself that it was actually great fun and you can still feel the buzz of achievement and confidence.

In front of you, the river now opens out into a huge lake. *'Finally, a break!'* your brain and your heart both say in unison, in agreement at last. You can see a number of small bays around the lake shores and the bobbing triangles of colour dotted around let you know that you're about to join other boats as you continue on your journey. Looks like things are going to change again!

The GROW section of your career is, not surprisingly, all about growth, so it is to be expected that you'll be tested and challenged along the way. You will always have to make hard choices which will mean that some doors close and you will never have the ability to see what was behind them, so it's best not to get distracted with the 'what ifs'. You can daydream about what might have happened with another choice, but you'll never be sure.

BE AS INFORMED AS YOU CAN BE

The only approach is to make the decision based on the best possible information you have at the time. This isn't always external information; remember to consider your own strengths and weaknesses and the potential for learning in each route.

It should be your priority to seek out as much detail as you can so that you can be confident in your decision and take responsibility for where it takes you. I should also point out that sometimes you'll want to go with the option that you know the least about – this could be because of gut feeling/intuition or perhaps because you've ruled out the others.

Our gut feelings are informed by thousands of tiny signals that our brain picks up on and processes against our previous experience and knowledge, so they're not as random at you may think. The important thing in any case is to take responsibility, make a decision and move forward.

FACE THE CHALLENGES

The other point to pick up on here is that no path is hazard-free. I guarantee that there will be challenges to every single project or role that you take on. It is an important skillset to be able to face a challenge, roll with the punches, get back up, improve and move on. Learning from your mistakes is a phrase that we hear when we're children and it is no less relevant when you're thirty than when you're three. The quicker you can learn and improve, the less chance that you'll get floored by that same issue a second time and the more confident you become. Every experience prepares you better for what is to come.

In my own career, I have a long list of occasions when I've made a decision and then had to learn and adapt very quickly in order to stay afloat. Once, as Head of Marketing and Communications, I successfully convinced the board that we needed to spend money on better photography to help with our brand image. I was sure that this was the right path to take to lift all of our marketing and communication efforts and to help position us in the top tier when it came to bidding for work.

I was delighted that my persuasion had worked; however, I was not a photographer and had no idea how to get the 'feel' that I was looking for. If you've ever dealt with creative people, they will normally ask for a brief and a list of exactly what is required. How they interpret this brief and how much of their own creativity they add into it depends very much on the individual.

I had three different options: use the photographer we had and try to get him to use a different style of photography, ask my network for recommendations, or find a photographer on my own.

I had a tight budget, no photography experience and not much time. I ruled out using our current photographer, but I wasn't confident enough just to engage someone else on recommendation, so I needed a different approach. I decided to go for option three and learn more about corporate photography. So I started my research.

I knew we needed more people-centric photography so I spent time researching brands who put people at the heart of their marketing. I went outside of my sector to find examples of what I wanted and to understand what gave certain photos their X-factor. Once I knew what I was looking for I could then research photographers and by checking their online portfolios I got a sense of the styles they liked to use. Had Instagram and Facebook been around then, this would probably have been a quick job, but they weren't so it took time and persistence!

Having narrowed it down to half a dozen potential professionals, my next step was to work out who would give me the creative input and personality that I needed for my project. I did this by asking them all to submit a creative bid for the work. By setting a mini competition I could gauge how interested they were in the work, how their creative process worked and what ideas they could bring to the table. Three photographers submitted a bid and from that I chose a wonderful photographer who subsequently worked with us for many years.

Another critical part of my learning was to go out with the photographer on the shoots and have an active conversation with him about what was working and what wasn't. He showed me his results as he went along and we could jump on opportunities as they appeared. It meant that in future when I was writing a photography brief, I could be very specific about what was needed, using the correct terminology and pre-empting questions I knew would be asked. It also meant some very long, cold days standing in the rain or grabbing employees before they started shifts at 5am – oh the glamour! I certainly appreciated my nice warm office much more the next day.

By committing to my promise, doing my research and learning as I went along, I felt confident that I had made the right choice and could defend my decisions should they ever have been questioned. Thankfully it didn't come to that and our new photography was very well-received, which not only helped the brand image, but also my reputation within the business.

LOOK LEFT AND RIGHT AS WELL AS STRAIGHT AHEAD

The final learning from this section is around your options. There will be very few occasions when there is only one choice in front of you. Sometimes it can be helpful to be very focused and this can guide you to the best decision; but there are also times when NOT taking the most obvious route is actually the best thing to do.

Learning and being curious are the best ways to get ahead, so if one route appeals to the side of you that wants an easy life because it's a simple repetition of what you've done before, then you should question if it's really the one that will benefit you the most.

Coincidence, chance, fate, luck... Whatever you may call an unexpected positive turn of events, it will only happen if you have made a decision to do something differently at some point. As the saying goes, 'Do what you've always done, get what you've always got.' It's without doubt the more challenging and scary option, but you don't get shareable social stories (or a fulfilling career) from always taking the safest choice!

By having the confidence in yourself and your abilities to be able to handle whatever comes up, you give yourself permission to experiment, try new things or take the left-field option. Life is a journey, not a destination.

GROW: EXERCISE 2

1. Write down a situation at work (real or imagined) that makes you squirm. What makes you feel REALLY uncomfortable and brings you out in cold sweats?

2. Now think about what skills or practise you would need to make that situation a bit less terrifying.

3. Next write down the steps you need to take to develop those skills or get that experience and the people who will help you or approve your plan.

There's no excuse now, you're all set. Make it happen.
Let's go back to the lake.

GROW: TAKE CONTROL OF YOUR WORKLOAD

As lovely as it is to get to the calm, less demanding water on the lake, you're immediately struck by how different this one is from the last one where you took your last break. It's much bigger, for one thing, and there are a number of other boats also sailing around it, both of which mean that you need to keep paying attention and can't fully switch off.

The concept of having other people to deal with isn't something that's come up before. You're certainly excited by the idea of talking to others, swapping stories and getting some tips, but there's an undeniable nagging feeling in your brain that this could complicate your journey or cause you some problems as well.

You don't have a lot of time to worry about it as the first boat is coming up alongside yours. The captain shouts to you that he saw you on the last part of the rapids and was impressed by how you handled them.

Your brain gives an appreciative nod and you heart gives a shy smile.

The next boat follows a few moments later with a third on its heels. They pull to a stop at almost the same time. Both captains shout in unison: *"I'm so pleased to see you, I've got a problem with my rudder (for one)/sail (for the other). Could you please help me? It's urgent, I need help now."* You are torn – who to help? You can't get on both boats at once and both issues are serious. You chose the broken rudder and jump abord. The broken-sail man glares at you and his boat limps slowly off towards another boat.

You get to work on the rudder and learn that the captain is a very experienced and interesting woman who has been sailing on a wide range of rivers in the past. She passes on some useful tips about dealing with rapids and how to spot dangers ahead before you get on top of them.

Noticing that you have an empty boat, she also passes on a spare oar and some food supplies, which you accept quickly and with many thanks. Your brain and your heart are also happily quiet, taking in what they need from this generous woman.

Just before you are ready to jump back into your boat, you ask the woman if she would be happy to meet up with you again a bit further down the river so that you can carry on the conversation. She agrees and mentions that she enjoys the distraction of talking to someone new, she never knows what she might learn!

For the next while, as you're crossing the lake, you come across a variety of people: some you help, some you have to say 'no' to, you pick their brains when possible and in one case you help a young sailor get back some supplies that another crew had stolen. It's also really interesting to watch the other boats and those manning them to see how they work: how they steer around others, send information signals, what equipment they have and how to make skippering a boat appear effortless.

Your brain gives you a little nudge as you cruise around: *"When are we going to head off again? Let's set a course to get off the lake".* Yes, good point. All these other boats can be as distracting as they are useful.

Just as you are getting ready to leave the lake, another boat pulls alongside and gets your attention. You're about to ignore it and pull away, when you hear the captain shout, *"I think we're heading in the same direction, do you want some company for a little while?"* While your brain is figuring out whether or not this would be a good idea, your heart has answered for you, *"Yes sure, it can get a bit lonely at times."*

Well, that's that then! Your brain sulks.

During the GROW phase, you'll notice that you get busier. Once you've completed a couple of projects and started to build a good reputation for yourself, you'll find that the number of people you interact with on a daily basis increases. You'll suddenly start getting emails asking for help with something or a meeting invite to bring you onto a new project team or questions from a colleague which take time to respond to. As with most things this is a double-edged sword, so balance is key.

You need to use your judgment and practise those negotiation, compromise, persuasion and humility skills that we touched in the ADAPT section (see page 26). You definitely do need the knowledge, support and variety which is offered by your colleagues. You definitely don't need to have an impossibly long or complex 'to-do' list, one-sided relationships or back-to-back meetings day in, day out. As we're striving to set the foundations for a healthy career, you need to be clear about what you're doing, why, who with and for how long. I'll give you some practical tips on these later in the chapter.

We go back to the Guiding Principle of 'Take Responsibility'. This time it's for your own workload. I guarantee that you are the only person who truly understands the extent and complexity of your daily job. While your manager is there for support and direction, he or she isn't a mind-reader, so if you are having issues with over-committing and are struggling to prioritise you need to say something. It's also not good enough to be a martyr, complain that you're working every night until 10pm, know you're exhausted, and say, *'That's just what the job needs'*. If that's what the job really needs, then it's completely unrealistic and needs to be reviewed. Look after your own wellbeing – the company isn't responsible for your health, you are!

This is a problem which really gets me worked up, so I make no apologies for being blunt about it. I have seen too many of my friends and colleagues work themselves into the ground because they thought it was expected of them or they were worried about flagging the problem, feeling it would reflect badly on them.

Let's walk this through. You're working on four different projects which are all with different people with a little overlap. They all have an influence on each other which is why you are involved in all of them, but each is still separate in the eyes of the business. So that means four sets of actions, four sets of priorities, four sets of meetings etc.

This is a classic case of an iceberg workload. Those working with you only see the small, twenty-five part that you are doing with them and none of the remaining seventy-five per cent. Your manager is aware of your involvement in each project but isn't involved him/herself, so therefore is relying on your account of them to keep him/her up to date.

If you're not careful, long hours and stressful days will become the norm, leading to exhaustion and a host of other issues, so please take it from someone who seen it before... Spot these signs and nip it in the bud.

Take responsibility for your own wellbeing. Talk to your manager honestly about your workload, give plenty of warning when things are starting to get too busy, build in a contingency plan for support and above all else, don't let the exception become the rule. One occasional weekend working is usual, four in succession, is not!

PEOPLE FOR SUPPORT

On a more positive note, other people are also the lifeblood of your career! They are mines of information, experience, support and friendship.

Aside from the obvious benefits to your life that work-friendships and positive working relationships have on your daily life, they are also critical to your healthy career. As on the lake, people at work can affect your life in positive ways that you can't anticipate and can't plan. Just as you are on your way through the organisation, so are they and you never know when your paths may cross or when you can help each other out.

The main learning at this point is that as well as the natural links that you make with people whom you click with, it's also worth making a specific effort to create links with people who are different from you. These people at various levels and from different departments can add layers of knowledge and add links to your network which you could never do on your own. Seek these connections out and actively engage with them.

UNCOMFORTABLE SITUATIONS

As you are GROWing in your career, you'll likely become responsible for delivering something substantial in this phase. It's at this point you will probably start to come across situations which you would previously have been cushioned from by a line manager or a bigger team in the ADAPT phase.

I'm talking about disappointment, conflict, rejection and humility and crucially, navigating office politics. Work colleagues are not usually our friends and they all have their own priorities, targets and pressure points. We can't choose them and we can't change them and they are not going to spend much time worrying about your reactions to things. Although this sounds harsh, it's often the honest truth. For lots of people, work is about prioritising themselves.

Work is the place where you will probably be the most exposed to negative and upsetting emotions and behaviours, because there are no filters. The overriding view normally is that 'it is what it is' and you just have to deal with it.

I'll just put in a quick disclaimer here and say that not every workplace or even every team is like this. I'm sure you have lots of examples of wonderful people you've worked with, but just be prepared that a more uncompromising environment is not uncommon.

It can come as a bit of a shock in the early stages of a career to be facing these testing emotions up-close; perhaps it's the first time you've ever been in these situations. Don't worry if it freaks you out initially. Learning how to understand and manage the people you work with, as well as your own reactions to negative feelings and events are skills you never stop building.

It's very hard not to take someone's negative reactions to something you have said or done personally and we will spend some time on this response a little later. For now, it's enough to be prepared for new and challenging situations and when they do arise to spend some time afterwards reflecting on your response and how the situation unfolded. This all adds to your internal view of our third Guiding Principle: 'Know Yourself'.

We're going to head back to your boat in a moment, but it's going to get tough, so strap in!

GROW: EXERCISE 3

1. Practise makes perfect. Think of three different people who regularly ask you take on more work or expect you to go above and beyond what you are prepared to do. Consider their personalities, how they work, what you know about them, how you've seen other people dealing with them successfully in the past and how they prefer to communicate.

2. Imagine a conversation with them or remember a past one in which you want(ed) to say 'no' but ended up doing the extra work. Create a conversation where you are able to successfully push back whilst still keeping a good professional relationship with them.

3. Practise it. Practise different variations. Practise how you would say it, email it, instant message it… You get the picture.

4. Then find a friend and work the scenario through with them or test your new skills on another colleague who perhaps isn't as influential or as senior as the person you're focusing on. The more you do it, the more comfortable you'll feel when the real moment arrives.

5. If you'd like some suggestions, look at the Practical Tips on page 106.

GROW: BE ALERT BUT NOT PARANOID

With your new friend in her boat alongside you, you set off out of the lake. Taking on the river in front of you, you're both swapping stories and passing on tips, laughing in the sunshine. It's interesting that you've got different skills and backgrounds and even though you're on the same river at the moment, your end goals are worlds apart. Your heart is happy for a bit of lightness and easy conversation and your brain is half paying attention while it also keeps you upright (and not making a fool of yourself in front of your new friend).

Suddenly the atmosphere changes. You both look

around you as you feel a shift in the air. Nothing is obvious but the hairs on the back of your neck are standing up and both your brain and your heart are fully alert. Something is going on.

Then you see it. A huge jaw filled with teeth pushes out of the water towards your friend's boat. Just short of the bow, an alligator smacks back into the water and its dark green, armour-plated body retreats. Your friend recovers her composure quickly as you shout at her to move as fast as she can.

As you're focused on her accelerating boat, you miss the whip of a tail that signals the return of the enormous alligator. Too late, you turn around at the sound of cracking wood, as you see the creature sink its teeth into the side of your boat, tipping it steeply to one side.

Your whole body is pumping with adrenaline as you hold on. Your brain is laser-focused on those jaws, waiting for the second when they release even slightly to get a better grip. You heart is predictably in your mouth! Then, as you see the alligator start to release its hold, you reach for the spare oar that your mentor gave you on the lake and jam it into its mouth. The shock of this sudden action scares the reptile and it sinks down into the water. Not waiting to find out if it's going to come back for another go, you try to coax your damaged boat as fast as you can downstream.

Luckily, a little way down the river you spot your friend waiting in a calm pool, her eyes worriedly fixed in your direction. Your boat is taking on water and you need to get somewhere safe where you can assess the damage. As you pull in, the sense of relief hits you like a bus and, shaking, you collapse to the bottom of your boat.

Working together and pooling your supplies, you are able to repair the boat and make it river-worthy again.

You've both had a nasty shock and care-free tone of the day has vanished. You sit in friendly silence while you digest what just happened. You realise that it's not just the river itself and the visible hazards that you have to watch out for, but also the ones hidden below the surface which can strike when you're not expecting it. Your brain sends you a warning: "*So perhaps a bit less chatting and laughing now and more paying attention...?*" Maybe. Although you're now more aware of what could happen and will certainly be more alert in future, you can't spend every moment staring at the water expecting monsters to appear, that's enough to drive anyone crazy.

At this point The Messy Middle is certainly living up to its name! The workplace is made up of humans, which naturally means that we get to experience ALL sides of human nature: the good and the bad. As I mentioned earlier, you can't change or choose your colleagues, so the key is to be prepared.

There's no doubt that you will have mostly positive relationships, which are beneficial and reciprocal. You'll have colleagues who will teach, support, help, trust, guide and back you and generally make work a pleasant place to be. We can't ignore the other side of the coin though. Jealousy, impatience, incompetence, fear, discrimination, dislike and distrust will all raise their ugly heads at along the path of your career.

Every situation will be different, as will your reaction, because you are human too – you're not programmed to give a specific response. Depending on who it is, what is happening, what the history is to the incident, who else is there, what mood you're in, whether you're hungry or not... Basically, every variable you can think of will change how a particular event plays out.

There are a few things that you can do in every circumstance which should help navigate complicated relationships or situations:

★ **Be aware.** Switch on your 'spidey-senses' and be as aware as possible of vibes, undercurrents of tension or unusual reactions in meetings. Often this is just a gut feeling as you catch a sideways look or a tone to someone's voice. Awareness is your biggest asset. If the issue is directly to do with you, then you can decide whether or not you want to address it or not at that point. If the issue seems to be between others, then it's probably not your place to dig deeper, but be aware that something is going on and keep tabs on it.

★ **Take early and direct action.** Addressing a difficult or awkward situation with a colleague is hard and uncomfortable, I get it, but believe me when I say that a short chat to get things out in the open, correct any misunderstandings and make amends is a better option every time than ignoring it and hoping it will go away. Take responsibility for your work relationships to make sure they are as productive and healthy as possible. You absolutely won't be best friends with everyone but figuring out how to work best with your team IS in your best interests.

★ **Tap into your empathy.** That huge alligator is just scared, hungry and defending his home, which you have strayed into with your noisy, disruptive and threatening boat ... so who is in the wrong here? Remember that there are two sides to every situation. Even if you can't catch yourself before you react in an angry, impatient or defensive way, you can certainly think about it afterwards and be the one to wave the white flag. Often someone's reaction isn't personal to you – they've probably got their own problems – but you've been the unfortunate one to trigger a reaction. Be inquisitive, show empathy, fix it (if you can) and move on. Don't let things haunt you.

★ **Use your support network.** It is undoubtedly upsetting when you have a run-in with someone or you find that a colleague is being less than supportive behind your back. Don't think that you have to suffer in silence. If their behaviour is just annoying and upsetting, then confiding in friends is very satisfying. If their behaviour is more serious and is verging on bullying, discrimination or harassment of any sort then don't shrug it off. This is not acceptable in any workplace and for any reason so speak honestly and quickly to a more senior person or someone who can help.

As we saw in the story, negative relationships at work drain our energy, sap our confidence and make us second-guess everything we do. They are not healthy, but they are inevitable. Try to build your resilience so that you approach them with a mature, confident, switched-on attitude and don't take everything too personally.

It's important to say that having a disagreement with someone at work is different from having a bad relationship with them. Women, it must be said, are often the worst at getting these two confused and can often shy away from any disagreement, believing that it destroys a relationship. There are historical, sociological and cultural reasons why this tends to be the case and it is to the detriment of working women that they struggle having positive disagreements.

We'll cover this a little more in the later chapter on Women at Work and if you're interested, Mary Portas covers this very thoroughly in her book, *Work Like A Woman*. For now, let's focus on why disagreement is healthy and necessary at work.

HEALTHY DISAGREEMENT

Apple didn't agree that Microsoft had all the answers. Air BnB didn't agree that we should only stay in hotels or B&Bs when we go away. Amazon didn't agree that long delivery times and complicated returns processes should be the norm when online shopping. All these companies disagreed on a fundamental level with the way things had always been done and they opened our eyes to a whole new world. They also became some of the biggest companies in the world because enough of the general public agreed with them.

While a disagreement at work may not be as profound as revolutionising the tech world or the holiday market, the same principle applies. Every single person is unique, with their own brain and set of influences. This means that we all process information, apply logic and solve problems in unique ways. It's amazing really that we ever agree on anything! The important part here is that usually it is the 'thing' that we have a different opinion on, not the 'person'.

When I've been mentoring younger managers, one particular situation comes up frequently, just like the following:

Claire presents an idea to a more senior colleague about restructuring a team project to try to increase its rate of progress, only for it to be dismissed with little explanation other than, *'No, I don't think that will work, it's too late to be making changes like that'*. Understandably this upsets Claire and she retreats quietly back to her desk and doesn't mention it again. By the time I speak to Claire, this situation has blown out of proportion in her head and she has told herself that this manager doesn't like her, won't listen to her and it will now be hard to carry on working with him. When I dig a little deeper to understand why the manager rejected the idea, Claire realises that actually she doesn't know. So we walk through a process whereby Claire goes back to the manager and tackles it a different way, so that at least she can understand what the issues are and can move on.

I suggest that she uses an approach based on **Acknowledgement > Inclusion > Reason**, something like: *I realise that my suggestion of XXX changes to the project aren't feasible <acknowledgement>, but I'd like to understand what you believe the issues are <inclusion> so that perhaps we can work on another solution, because at the moment I'm concerned that we're not going to hit our deadline <reason>.*

By using this formula, the aim is to avoid a confrontation and understand the situation better so that your next suggestion is a huge success. The point is that when you see this from the outside, you can clearly see that there's a high chance that the manager has no problem with Claire as a person, it's just that he thought her suggestion wouldn't work; but it can be harder to make this distinction when you're in the midst of it.

If you notice yourself sliding into endless negative self-talk, try to be your own best friend and ask: *Is this really, 100% true? Do you have actual evidence that this is the case?* As you can imagine, often that proof doesn't exist, so it's time to leave those thoughts behind and move on.

GROW: EXERCISE 4

1. When was the last time that you had a run-in with a colleague?

2. With some time and hindsight, walk it through and try to see it from an outside point of view.

3. Tap into your empathy and consider if there are other explanations for their behaviour? Was there a reason why you reacted as you did? If someone else was observing you from a distance, how might they have described the event?

4. What would you do differently a second time around to give a more positive result?

GROW: TAKE TARGETED, PRECISE ACTION

You and your friend move off back into the main channel, chatting about this and that. Gradually a familiar rushing and roaring sound gets louder and louder as you move forward. Your brain clicks into a higher gear and your heart leaps as it recognises the noise – rapids, big ones! You share an excited glance with your friend as you both realise at the same time. The atmosphere is different from before, you're both experienced in dealing with rapids now and know that this is going to be fun. You're rested, full of energy and looking forward to experiencing the high you get from tackling these tricky obstacles. *'Let's do this!'* your brain says.

There's no hesitation this time, you both hit the rapids together at speed. You naturally work together; shouting help to each other, pointing out hazards and supporting each other. The teamwork is faultless and thanks to this you both have the most successful, enjoyable run yet. Your brain is 100% focused on putting everything you've learnt into practise and keeping you upright, ignoring anything else. Your heart is telling you that these rapids are only ever short, so you need to throw everything you have at them and take all the fun and learning you can while you're here. *'Live for the moment!'* your heart cries.

As you slow down towards the end of the boiling torrent, you're both exhausted but the smiles that fill your faces tell the true story. You're in your element; you've found a path that you love, you've learnt the techniques, battled the challenges and created a support network. You've taken responsibility for your career and now you're getting the pay-back.

You're not so worried about the paths ahead now because you have the confidence and self-belief to back yourself. You take a deep, slow breath in and out and raise your eyes up to the horizon. As you focus, pleasure floods through you, there it is, your palace is back in view. You'd been so caught up in the last few challenging miles that you'd not even glanced in that direction. You're back on course and you find deep satisfaction in knowing that all the efforts of last two stages have brought you within striking distance of the palace. Your heart and your brain give each other a high five. Not far now.

The final challenge of the GROW phase is also your chance to show just how much you've grown. It's your most demanding, complicated, high-profile piece of work to date and the good news is that it feels like a natural progression. You feel ready. You know that you will need to draw on all the skills, tips and energy reserves that you've built over the last few months to make a real success of this.

There are a few key tips to making that success a realistic and tangible thing:

KNOW WHAT SUCCESS LOOKS LIKE FOR YOU

Of course, the most obvious measure of success is the delivery of the end result – whatever that may be. But in reality, that success is multi-layered because every single person who is involved in the piece of work has a slightly different view of it. Any piece of work impacts people differently, either from a personal or a business perspective. This means that no matter the outcome, you'll never please everyone or meet 100% of the expectations, often because some expectations are pure fantasy! The lesson here is to take control of the story from your side.

Be crystal clear about what success looks like for you on a professional and personal level. For example, integrating a new project management tool into the business could have the professional success factors of:

★ The old system is switched off successfully without any data loss.

★ Eighty per cent of the core user group adopts the new system within two months.

★ Accurate monthly reports are now automatically emailed to the relevant directors.

The personal success factors could be:

★ Building relationships with a new team.

★ Developing your delegation skills.

★ Testing out a new project-management technique to deliver the system.

You can also have other success goals attached to piece of work: perhaps getting the opportunity to practise your presentation skills, getting some air-time with an influential senior person, or taking the chance to go to a conference associated with the project to pick up best-practise and expand your network.

You can hopefully see where I'm going with this: success comes in many shapes, sizes and colours, so make sure you've got a few different goals outlined. It almost goes without saying that not everything you plan will go perfectly, so by seeing the project from a range of angles, you have a number of ways to measure its success.

BE SIMPLE, DIRECT AND CONSISTENT

Anyone should be able to jump into one of your meetings or read some of your communications and understand exactly what's going on at a high level. Remember that you are always competing for your colleagues' attention and time; even in meetings they will get distracted with other messages and emails flooding in. It's only natural to be more interested by things that are easier on our brain and we need to be exposed to the same information many times before we actually remember it. You need your work to be easy to take in, understand, act on and pass on. Often those involved in the project will change as things progress and you need each new person to be able to get up to speed as quickly and efficiently as possible.

GET THE BASICS RIGHT

This is such an easy step, but so many people forget to do it and it can have significant consequences to your success later on. When you're agreeing to take on a new piece of work you should always ask **what/why/how/who/when/how much** to establish as much information as you can right at the start.

You need to be able to paint a picture of what you

are being asked for so that you can check it with the person who's asking for it. I've often seen it happen that the person asking for the work doesn't always know the answers, which is also a good prompt for them to check their own understanding of what they are asking for. Sometimes when they hear a request played back to them, it is clear that there some conflicts that they hadn't thought of.

Here's a small example of what can happen when these details aren't confirmed at the start. I was working as part of a digital marketing team and apps suddenly exploded onto the scene. Even in the traditional B2B sectors, every company who thought of themselves as 'innovative' was shouting about their latest app. I was aware of apps and used them a lot in my personal life, but I'd never been involved in developing one before.

As at the start of all new technologies, there's a lot of noise and dramatic reaction from a few people in a company, but the majority don't know much about them and it's very much a 'figure it out as you go' mentality. That's fine if you've got endless budget and time, but in reality, working blind is challenging. I was told that the CEO wanted an app. When I asked what for, I was told something vague like, 'Just to help with communication and brand awareness'. In hindsight, this **wasn't** a reason to have an app and an app was very unlikely to ever fulfil this need – but at the time that was all I had to work with, so I went with it.

Of the core six questions above, as well as the **What** (an app) I found out the answer to the last two: **When:** in two-months. **How much:** as little as possible, certainly no size of budget that would require any high-level sign-off.

In short, I had to create an app to tell an unknown audience something about the business that they may or may not be interested in, using an unknown technology in two months' time on a shoestring budget. What could possibly go wrong?!

I'll spare you the painful details and summarise: it was a stressful, frustrating, enraging two months which ended up in an app that updated people on company news. Completely useless! No one used apps for news updates (even in the early days) and we didn't have the internal processes in place to even update the news in the app easily or regularly.

Unsurprisingly, after the launch, very few people downloaded it and even most of the marketing team forgot about it. We had delivered what had been asked for – but because we hadn't established the answers to the other fundamental questions, it was ultimately a waste of time, money and energy.

So, let's look at each of the questions:

What: Make sure you are clear in your head about EXACTLY what it is you need to deliver and to what level of detail.

Why: What is the problem you're being asked to solve, the solution you're investigating or the purpose behind the request?

How: Think about relevant technologies, processes, teams, people, locations, digital, hard-copy, in-person, remote... etc.

Who: Who is your audience(s)? How big is it?

How much do you know about them? Will there be a staged release to a number of different audiences or everyone at once?

When: You need to know important dates that will create milestones for your piece of work. That's not just the end-delivery date, but other events which will dictate progress or impact your project in some way.

How much: There could be a finite budget, but more often than not one of the first steps will be to get a quote for the work. This could be in internal-hours-worked if money is not changing hands. It's important to understand where the red lines are and what the expectations are for the ROI (return on investment) of the project, as this should be more relevant than the cost. A project which costs £100,000 but which delivers savings or income of £300,000 is money well-spent, whereas spending £10,000 on a badly designed project which gives nothing back, is money down the drain, even if the 'budget' was less to start with.

There will usually be levels of expenditure too, different options depending on the quality/time decisions which are driving the piece of work, so be prepared to look beyond the obvious solution to find other methods which may yield a better result. You could well change a decision on an initial budget if you can prove that a larger, longer-term investment is actually a sounder choice.

GROW: EXERCISE 5

1. Do the 'Basics' test **(what/why/how/who/when/how much)** for a significant piece of work that you're currently doing.

2. Where are the gaps?

3. Go and fill them!

GROW: PRACTICAL TIPS

GET A COACH AND/OR A MENTOR

Before we go any further, there is a difference! Both can be inside and/or outside your business, depending on how big the organisation is that you work for and if there are structures in place for this kind of support.

A coach tends to be a person who will support you with a particular problem or skill that you want to develop. You'll normally have a number of sessions with them for a defined length of time. After which, you'll feel stronger and more confident with that skill. The work will be done by you and they will prompt you to find your own answers to your questions. Often the coach doesn't need specific experience of your business sector or job type to help you, it's more about focusing on and understanding the underlying skills, behaviours or habits.

A mentor is a longer-term relationship. This person will usually be more senior to you and will have a different (wider) network which they could use to help you. The aim of the mentor is to always be in your corner and to help you to become the best version of you. They understand what you want from your career and will help you to get it. This relationship is often more reciprocal as both the mentor and mentee can learn from each other while they work through challenges together. The mentor usually has experience in the sector and/or job role of the mentee and therefore can act in an advisory role, suggesting solutions or approaches for the mentee to try.

Within your business?
There are pros and cons of working with someone within your business in this way. Pros are that they understand the environment and the people very well and so can give you very targeted, specific, practical advice and help. Particularly in the mentoring relationship, they may be able to open doors for you which wouldn't be possible for an external person. Cons are that you may feel a slight resistance to being completely open with them for fear of something 'negative' coming out which could harm your chances of progressing within the company.

In my opinion it comes down to two things: do you see a long-term future in your business for you? Is there a scheme in place or do you have someone in mind who you'd like to approach? If the answer is 'Yes' and 'Yes', then I think it's worth a shot to find a mentor and/or coach within your business, if it's big enough.

If not...

Look externally

Often a great place to start for mentors are the 'Chartered Institutes' or governing bodies for your particular specialism or area of interest. I'm a mentor for the Chartered Institute of Marketing and have mentored and coached people from all sectors and levels when they have a question about marketing/digital or are stuck in their careers.

You can also find interest groups on LinkedIn which may be able to connect you to individuals who could help. Don't forget about your alumni from university or business school; these groups are an often-missed resource but can be full of people happy to help a fellow graduate of the same school.

There are also thousands of coaches with various specialisms who pop up with a simple Google search. You'll need to do the due diligence on them yourself.

At Find Your Wings, we offer both coaching and mentoring for individuals and business. Between us and our expert network, we have at our fingertips the experience to work across a huge range of sectors and disciplines. Just have a look at our website (**www.findyourwings.co.uk**) or drop me a message **hello@findyourwings.co.uk**, There is also more information about Find Your Wings at the back of the book.

MANAGING YOUR WORKLOAD: SAYING 'NO'

Saying 'no' in a situation where you are the more junior person is an art form, one that needs to be practiced! You won't always get the outcome you want, but try to reflect on every occasion that you do say it and make a note of the responses and the outcome. Also notice when you really SHOULD have said no and consider why you didn't; if you were given the situation again, how could you have turned it around?

In many cases, the person who is asking you to do something may not know the full story: your full workload, your skill set, your other commitments, the full implication of what they are asking you to do, the dependencies/impacts of you taking it on, what else is happening elsewhere in the business, that you have holiday coming up, etc. They could also just be trying to get rid of something they don't want to do and so are just asking the first person they see/think of. If any or all of these things are true, then the only way to tackle this is by communication.

Let's work this through... Before you commit to anything, do two things: **BUY yourself some time** and **FIND all the information.** Once you have these two things, if you want/need to say 'no', work through these questions:

★ Why is this person asking you specifically? Are you really the ONLY person who could do this?

★ What are the alternatives to you doing it?

★ What are the deadlines? Are they REAL deadlines?

★ Are you allowed to delegate?

★ If you say yes, what other project or responsibility does it replace?

★ What would happen if you said yes but then didn't deliver? This is often worse than saying no in the first place!

★ Who is the person who is asking in relation to you and within the organisation? Do you have support from anyone else if you push back?

★ Can you say yes, but set your own terms as to the deliverables?

Once you've decided that you are going to say no, there are ways of saying it without it sounding like a hard 'no'.

A no that's a 'yes but later'
Yes that sounds like a great opportunity, I'd love to help but I can't really get involved until XXXX, so if that works, great, if not – then I'll just catch up with it later or pick up the opportunity next time.

A helpful no
I just can't take that on at the moment, but I'd be happy to recommend someone else or an agency/freelancer etc if you'd like some support.

That's not really something I can commit to at the moment but I've heard that there's a similar or related project happening elsewhere in the business which it may be useful for you to link up with.

A yes but with pushback
Yes that sounds like something I should be doing, but I do

have some clashes with other priorities at the moment, so perhaps we could sit down with (my manager/other the person setting the projects) and work out what gets de-prioritised so that I can take this on?

A no that protects your reputation
I'm sorry but I just don't have capacity at the moment to take on anything else and I'd hate to agree to it and then let you down or give you something which isn't a standard I'm happy with.

ASK FOR HELP

Asking for help in itself isn't a hard thing to do and it's strange that it causes us so many problems. The challenge is more about the perception of the request, than the actual request itself. We tie ourselves up in knots worrying what the other person will think of us; will we seem like we don't know what we're doing? Will we appear weak that we can't work it out on our own? Will it seem like time-wasting or will it bother the person we're asking?

The obvious answer is that you will never know until you ask and if you can't progress with something without help, then asking someone is inevitable. So, it's now more about HOW you ask then the request itself.

Put yourself in the shoes of the person to whom you're going for help. Yes, they will probably be busy. Yes, you may not be top of their priority list, but it's also true that it is flattering being asked to help someone, as the assumption is that this person has knowledge or skills that you need. It's also a much more attractive request if in helping you, there is a benefit to the other person.

You have to be master of your own fate. No one is going to check in with you every few hours to see if there's anything you need help with, unless you tell someone that there's a problem, how will they know?!

To summarise: the best way to ask for help is ... actually asking. Have the confidence that if it is a genuine request no one is going to reject you entirely. Make it as easy as possible for the person you are asking to say yes. Explain to them why you have chosen to come to them, be realistic about the time frames that you need the help in, be very specific in exactly what you need and demonstrate how it could benefit them, if that's an option.

Now we need to address what happens if the person says that they can't help you. Try not to take it personally and instead use some compassion – there may be things happening within the life of this person which are preventing them from helping you. So, after thanking them for their time, it's also worth asking this person if there is anyone else who they can recommend you speak to for help. Sometimes people do U-turns at this point as they realise that they really are the best person to help and by going to someone else they lose any control of the outcome. It also defuses any possible worry from the other person that they can't help you, as they can still point you in a helpful direction.

DELEGATE

Everyone has their own style of management and leadership, which means that everyone has their own style of delegating. Delegating is fundamentally about trust, so people handle it in different ways depending on their willingness and ability to trust others to do work for them. It's a case of matching the person who is best placed to do the work (in terms of skill) with the time available (the person's time as well as the deadline) and then judging the approach based on their relationship with you. You can judge from your own experience the techniques you've seen which have been the most effective and those which have not led to a positive experience.

Delegating is an important skill to understand and practise. When we're thinking about a successful, long-term career, it's going to help you manage your workload, deliver the goods AND keep your stress levels under control. It's all about finding your style and working with those around you. Here are some practical steps:

1. Make a decision: Figure out exactly what can be delegated and what you need to own yourself. Choose the best person. Who is best placed to help you? What skills/experience do you need to stand the best chance of the work being done well?

2. Be the lighthouse. The person who you're delegating to needs to know that you will be there to support them. You need to give very clear guidance on the what/why/how/who/when/how much answers.

3. Allow for learning and failure. Things go wrong and people make mistakes … for many, many different reasons. Accept this, understand why it has happened, learn from it, take time with the person at the centre of it and emphathise with them ... and then move on. You may have to take the heat for someone else's mistakes, but that's the downside of delegating. You're all in it together.

4. Let them be the hero. Taking credit for someone else's work is possibly one of my biggest personal bugbears, and I don't think I'm alone. If someone has done a good piece of work for you, let them shine. They have worked hard for it. We all need those moments.

Unfortunately, especially in the early part of a career, you may find that someone has taken credit for YOUR work. This can lead to resentment, so it's best to try to address it. As tempting as it is to try to call this person out in public so that everyone understands the origins of the idea, this could backfire as it can come across as petty. Better to add your voice in support and then offer some more detail or extend the idea further. By agreeing that your colleague has made a good point, you show support for him/her and then by enhancing it, you add value. Win-Win!

COMMUNICATE (THE 'WHAT' AND THE 'HOW')

We all see the world very differently. In our many personal and professional roles, we will often find ourselves in situations where there can be several different perspectives or opinions around the same table. The ability to see someone else's perspective can go a long way in helping to explain their actions and views. Luckily someone is here to help us with this understanding.

Gretchen Rubin has done some really interesting work on the 'four tendencies' framework which outlines how people respond to expectations (from themselves and from others). The four types of personality that she describes are: Upholder, Questioner, Obliger and Rebel. The different tendencies shown by these four types explain why you will meet so many different reactions to the same information, situation or request at work. We can see within ourselves elements of all four 'types', to differing degrees, but we usually have one stronger preference:

★ **Upholders** want to know what should be done and respond readily to outer and inner expectations.

★ **Questioners** want justifications. They will question all expectations and will only meet an expectation if they think it makes sense.

★ **Obligers** meet outer expectations, but struggle to meet expectations they impose on themselves, so therefore need accountability.

★ **Rebels** resist all expectations and want freedom to do something their own way.

There's a free quiz on her website if you'd like to see where you sit. The web address is at the end of the book.

Rubin's work shows us how we all react differently when asked to do something or when an expectation is set for us, which is directly relatable to the challenges we saw in the delegating section above. It also demonstrates that when communicating to a group of people, particularly if it's a team that is meant to be delivering a project, the type of information that you give needs to be flexible. What you communicate needs to be clear and precise enough for Responders. It needs to be detailed enough for the Questioners. It needs to have a clear structure and actions for the Obligers and finally it needs to have enough stretch and scope to give space to the Rebels.

In the ADAPT section on Learning and Development, we looked at the varied learning styles that we all have (see page 50). This shows us that everyone has a preference when it comes to how they take in new information, whether that be by reading something, doing something or listening to someone. So, it's not just the WHAT that is important in communication, but also the HOW.

Effective communication of what you're doing and why can seem like an endless and thankless task, but it's crucial for the approval of and participation in your piece of work. Make sure you can use all the communication platforms that you have available to you and decide how you're going to use them.

★ It may be that all information is held in one place, but updates go out over several channels with links back to the central store.

★ Remember that not everyone has the same mother-tongue/language as you, so keep your written text in plain, easy-to-understand, short sentences.

★ Explain all acronyms, abbreviations and slang.

★ Add in links to anything additional which could help to expand or explain your subject.

★ Use a combination of text, diagrams, photos, charts, numbers to show things in different ways.

★ Give solid reasons as to why you're doing something or asking for something and use your opinion wisely.

★ Give different options for input or reaction.

★ Keep core messages consistent and repeat them EVERY time you communicate.

★ Make sure communication is regular and reliable and the history can be found if someone needs to dig back (this can also save your skin if you're being criticised for not passing on a crucial piece of information which you had in fact communicated).

★ Check-in with people. Go outside of your immediate team on a regular basis and see how much of your message is getting out to your core group of stakeholders, this will very quickly reveal how well you are communicating and if anything needs to change.

Effective communication is a skill in itself and although we notice when it's not done well, we often don't appreciate when it IS being done well. As we are all individuals, you'll never be able to communicate exactly the way that every person would prefer so you'll always hear grumbling, but if you follow those tips above you'll be doing well.

PICK YOUR BATTLES

Projects or issues that we feel strongly about can really push our buttons and lead us to behave in emotional and spontaneous ways. While it's important that you stand up for what you believe in; someone who is highly charged and emotional on every issue loses credibility and the effectiveness of their arguments lose their power. If there is an issue or an opinion that you really want to address, try to take a breath, step back and consider these points:

★ What do I want to get out of this conversation?

★ What do I want to get out of taking a stance on this issue as a whole?

★ Who am I talking to? What's my relationship with them and what part do they play in my day-to-day work life as well as my future work life?

★ What's the potential fall-out from my opinion? Who will I hurt/impact?

★ Is it just my opinion or can it be backed up by

facts? Do I know what these are or should I do some checking first? Am I sure I'm right?

★ To what extent will taking a stand on this potentially alter the outcome … and is it worth it?

Remember: sometimes it is worth conceding the battle to win the war. Try to think longer-term, for you and the business, before jumping into every contentious issue with both feet.

That said, it doesn't mean that you need to melt into the background. If something IS important to you and you feel very strongly about it, then do make yourself heard; just chose your platform and your timing wisely. Large, group Zoom calls are not the place!

Giving yourself the space to think and reflect, even for five minutes, could make a huge difference to your reaction and therefore to how others perceive you and your credibility in the business.

REASSESS THE VALUE OF YOUR NEGATIVE VOICE

We've seen throughout our river journey that it's quite normal to have conflicting 'voices' swirling around your head. In this instance, we have the Heart with its positive, pro-active, 'give it a go' energy, while the Brain has been injecting the negative, nagging, doom-filled opinions into every scenario. This negative voice, in particular, can get quite loud at times.

When your own negative voice is challenging or questioning you, it can feel stressful and irritating. Depending on our mood and temperament we probably flip between trying to ignore it and believing it entirely; with neither approach providing very positive results. However, our brains are pretty clever and self-sabotage doesn't end up benefitting anyone, so perhaps there is another way to consider it.

This voice can also be viewed as your drive and imagination trying to get your attention, provoking you to keep growing and learning. It's driven by enthusiasm and ambition. Sometimes you may feel resistance to it, as your brain is doing its job of keeping you safe and avoiding any risk and unknowns. But ultimately, exploring the ideas this voice is giving you will add to your journey rather than stifle it.

It's also good to remember that there is safety in the known and comfortable. At times we need to sink into that and enjoy the feeling of just being happy with where are, proud of what we've achieved so far and in a more restful state. Listen to the voice but don't be its puppet.

The negative voice which has the most destructive power is the one which only ever sees the worst-case scenario. This voice is driven by fear. Once again, our clever brain is trying to just keep us safe. Evolution did a good job of giving us a reflex which stops us walking into oncoming traffic or jumping off a cliff edge; it definitely has its uses. But the point at which it stops becoming useful is when it brings up our shame, or our insecurities or our phobias to stop us acting.

The real kicker is that this voice really ramps up a gear whenever we stray out of our comfort zone. Just when you want some words of encouragement and positivity to propel you forward, this voice chimes up with, 'Really? You? Do that? Are you kidding me? You're much to lazy/stupid/unreliable/ugly/boring to be any good at that! Why are you even trying it? You know what happened last time you tried something new, it was a complete flop. You know you'll fail, right? And then where will you be? You'll have wasted your time and proven how stupid you are for believing that YOU could do THAT! Just give it up now and save us all the heartache.'

Awful, isn't it? Imagine how shocked and outraged you would be if someone said that to one of your friends. Yet we allow ourselves to let this toxic voice fill our heads and take us over. It stops us dead in our tracks. We retreat. Here we see the beginnings of imposter syndrome (see page 167) which can, if we let it, creep into every area of our life.

But look at it from arms-length and with a growth mindset (rather than a defeatist one) and you get a different perspective. If you heard your friend being spoken to in that way, perhaps over her idea of taking her painting from a hobby to a profession, you'd step back and rationalise it with her.

You'd say something like, "Right, so taking your painting to the next level is a big step. Yes, you will need to change your routine to give yourself the time to do it and yes, you will need to invest in some new equipment. You'll even need to find a space which suits you to paint in. BUT, everyone who has ever seen your work thinks you're very talented. You don't need to give up your job initially to do it so you're not risking anything financially and it brings you joy and peace when you're painting. What a wonderful gift to have! The rational voice comes so easily when you're a little removed from the toxic one. It's gives space for a reality check and to turn the mental assault into valid questions to be considered with interest.

This is my greatest lesson for dealing with our internal negativity: give it the space it needs to 'vent' but don't get too close. You'll never outrun fear, it's part of our make-up, so don't think you can just ignore it or push it away, it just comes back stronger. It's like the toddler who wants your attention. If you ignore him, the little cry that started as a quiet 'Mummy' to get your attention escalates into a toy-throwing tantrum with fists pumping and little legs stomping. The only way to really handle him is to give him space to talk and actively listen to what he has to say. The same goes for your negative voice. Let it get all of the fear and 'what ifs' out of its system and when it has finished, consider the information as if you were hearing it about a friend. Lean towards the positive side, acknowledge the risks, point out the blatant lies and exaggerations and then move on with whatever insights you have gained.

Be your own best friend. Remember that, ultimately, you're going to be ok. You have people who love and admire you just as you are. You are stronger, more resilient and more creative than you could ever imagine. You are enough.

THE WHEEL OF PERSPECTIVE

This is a useful tool to have up your sleeve when you start to feel caught up in a cycle of negative thoughts. The idea is to force you to think about all the other possible angles to your issue and break you out of obsessing over just one.

Let's take a common work problem to show how to put it into practise: *I disagreed with my manager in a meeting and he hasn't spoken to me about it since, I feel like he now holds a grudge and I don't want to face him.*

Now draw a circle and split it into 6 segments like a wheel.

Write your original issue in one segment.

Then in the other segments explore other explanations:

For our example, in the other segments you could write:

1. I haven't had chance to see my manager since the meeting, so I don't actually know if he's angry.

2. He replied to another message about something else so he's not ignoring me.

3. When we've disagreed in the past, he's never reacted badly to it.

4. Perhaps there's something else going on with him which means our disagreement isn't top of his mind.

5. He could think that we settled it all within the meeting and therefore there's nothing left to discuss.

The aim is to give some perspective and objectivity to your situation and help you act more rationally. So rather than a knee-jerk emotional outburst in an email, perhaps you could find a reason to follow up on something else from that meeting with him in person and then do a 'temperature check' on the thorny issue to see where things lie.

Let's move into the final stage of our journey. Are you ready to THRIVE?

THRIVE

- THE JOURNEY NOT THE DESTINATION

You're content. The satisfaction of getting this far feels good and you allow yourself to enjoy the achievement. The daily tasks of manning the boat come easily to you and you find pleasure in being skilled at managing it. The relationship you have with your friend has become easy, reliable and fun. You both appreciate each other's strengths and have each other's back when it gets tough.

You'd think that your brain and heart would be equally as satisfied. But they're not. Because you're now so expert in navigating the boat they are less and less engaged. The rest of your body has taken over and so much has become automatic. This has given them both space to think. Your heart is a little bored. *'Where's the action? The adventure? The next new thing?'* Your brain, although approving of the steady and reliable routine, keeps wondering when it will all end. 'Surely this easy life will be disrupted any time now?' It starts looking for the potential catastrophes in every small action, creating scenarios that just don't exist in an effort to give it some purpose.

Luckily, the river is wiser than us all. It knows apathy and boredom can set in and it doesn't want us to get to the palace in this mood.

It's your ears that first pick up the changes to the river channel up ahead. There are sounds like there's more rushing water, something bigger coming up. It's not the churning, angry torrent that you've learnt comes with rapids, it's different. New. *'That's more like it!'* Your heart suddenly perks up. *'I knew it, I knew it, I knew it!'* your brain declares, although its interest has been piqued too.

You glance at your friend and her body position tell you that she's noticed it too. She catches your eye and just shrugs. She's just as clueless. Only one way to find out, you've got to keep going.

The haze over the river ahead starts to clear as you approach and the details of what's in front of you start to reveal themselves. Whoa! This is VERY new. Your eyes focus on not one, but three significant river courses ahead of you. They are each comfortably as large as the river you've been on up to now and each hold their secrets close, not revealing much of what lies ahead. The only thing that's certain is that you HAVE to make a decision. Which way?

Your brain and your heart snap out of their stunned silence and start doing what they both do best – talking. Your brain is desperately trying to get you focus on facts and reality, with a healthy dose of negativity thrown in for good measure: *'Let's look at each river course. Which appears to be the easiest? Which has the most direct route to the palace? We're good at doing what we know, let's choose the option that carries on that path.'* Your heart is quick to jump in: *'Oh come on, we've all been bored for a while. We needed something new to fire us up again – this is perfect. Take the route that looks the most interesting. I reckon go right… No, wait a minute… Go left… Actually, maybe I can see some interesting twists and turns in the central channel. Oh no, that's just a tree moving… I stick with left… hmmmm… or…'*

You take heed of both voices; they both have something useful to offer but neither is giving you a clear plan. You slow the boat right down and motion to your friend to do the same. She glides in alongside you. It quickly becomes clear that not only do you each need to think about what YOU would like to do individually, you now also have the decision of whether to go forward together or separately. This has just made things 100% harder. You think back to the foundations of what you've learnt: Take Responsibility, Show Empathy and Know Yourself.

You both sit down on the bottom of your boats and float in silence for a while, lost in your thoughts, weighing up the options. You think back to the journey you've taken so far. You couldn't have predicted most of what happened, the bad or the good. The only certain thing is that you were ok. You got through it all. You found what you needed at the time, either from others or within yourself. You're actually quite a capable and resilient person, come to think of it! Your heart and your brain both nod their agreement at this thought.

You have faith that you'll get to your palace, but you're no longer obsessed with it as a fixed idea. You're open to the fact that along the journey it may change shape. You suddenly realise that it's the journey itself which you live every day. That is what shapes you, challenges you and rewards you. The palace will only be yours for a moment in time. You still want to get there and achieve that goal, but you're now more sure that you'll get to it whichever river course you take. Of course, you'd love your friend to come along with you but you're also certain that you'll meet other wonderful people along the way. You're going to pick a course and she needs to pick hers. If you chose the same or different channels, that's ok. You're excited by the new challenge whichever way it goes.

You choose to go right.

This is the last stage of your journey, but don't start thinking that this is the end of your career. Remember, you're aiming to get to the palace, which is **one** of your big career goals. Once you've got to the palace, you've only got a visitor's pass, you're not moving in permanently. It's a wonderful moment that should be recognised and celebrated, but the river carries on flowing.

It is the whole journey that makes up your career, not just the palace. It's all the experiences, the learnings, the highs, the lows, the relationships, the disasters and the triumphs. Don't feel bound to your palace forever once you get there, that is a direct route to boredom and frustration, instead your career aspirations need to carry on growing with you. At some point your boat will be calling you to jump back in and head off for another palace you hadn't foreseen and your heart won't be able to resist it. So, embrace the river and all it can teach you.

But for now, we're still in the final stage of this part of our journey and THRIVE is all about pulling on your big pants and standing tall with your shoulders back and your head held high. Remember our three Guiding Principles: Take Responsibility,

Show Empathy and Know Yourself. By this point you've been practising them for a while and hopefully they are feeling more natural. You have confidence in yourself and your abilities which means you can **take responsibility** for your actions, decisions and opinions. You can use and **show empathy**, even when it's hard. You **know yourself** and can listen to the cues your brain and your heart give you. You've also set up some positive, sustainable routines and behaviours which give you the energy, focus, resilience and humility you need to manage most situations that are thrown at you. You're doing really well!

When it comes to the three principles, they may also be helpful when people come into your life who change your thinking and your priorities; they could be a child or someone who needs your care. They can give you a structure for reflecting on your ambitions and the challenges ahead and help you adapt.

In this stage of your career, there are still more tests to navigate, decisions to make and skills to learn and practise. We'll be having a look at some of the obstacles that you could come up at this stage, such as imposter syndrome, unconscious bias and the authority gap. The stakes get higher as you get further along, but you're also better equipped to deal with them. You've got everything you need you move forward.

I want you to really get into the THRIVE mindset, so let's do a five-minute exercise.

Sit down with your eyes closed and imagine you have a pair of wings attached to the point between your shoulder blades. These wings are unique to you. They reflect your personality. They can be dainty fairy wings, powerful eagle wings, stealthy bat wings or maybe you'd prefer to invent your own entirely. Add some colour. Imagine their shape. What are they made from?

Most of the time these wings stay folded neatly between your shoulder blades, you can feel them nestled there securely. Your wings hold within them your confidence, your strength, your bravery and your knowledge. You can tap into these whenever you need them.

Now, stand up. Close your eyes and imagine your wings unfolding behind you. You can feel their weight and when you move you hear the air move around you differently. Now come back to the room.

I imagine you stood a little straighter, held your head a little higher, pushed your shoulders back and your chest out. This is what your wings do for you. Just this act of finding your wings and opening them up allows all that positive energy to flow through your body.

You can use this any time you need a boost: perhaps when you're giving a presentation or about to have a difficult conversation or need to speak in public. Whenever your stomach is in a knot and your negative voice is starting to kick in, concentrate on your wings. Opening them will give you the strength and focus you need to keep going.

THRIVE: CHANGE IS LIFE

Change is life. Change for the better, for the worse, for something different, temporary or permanent. You can resist it or welcome it. Try to control it or embrace the uncertainty. Depending on your mood and the situation you may go through all of these when working through it.

As you get more experienced in your career there will certainly be 'fork in the road' decisions which will have significant impact on your life. At these moments I have two pieces of advice:

1. Buy yourself some time. Make sure you get some 'lying in the bottom of the boat' time just to let thoughts, options, choices and feelings float through you. Tap into your brain and your heart and see what they are saying to you. Listen and reflect.

2. Go back to your three Guiding Principles:
   a. Take responsibility for your decision. Don't let anyone make it for you. Whatever you decide to do, you need to be able to confidently say, 'I am doing this because...' That reason doesn't have to satisfy anyone but you.
   b. Show Empathy. Unless you are a hermit,

your decision will impact others. The extent and the importance of that impact will obviously vary and whether those people are within your inner circle also makes a difference. It's much more significant to your family if you decide to move to another country than it is to your neighbour. However, having empathy for your loved ones is different to letting them dictate what you should do. Look back to the first point about taking responsibility.

c.Know Yourself. During your thinking time, try to step back and think: which route 'feels' the most like me? Which gets me most excited? Which will I ultimately get the most benefit from? Which one sticks closer to my values?

There are a few ways you can do this. I love to write things down and use language (no surprise there!) so for me, a blank sheet of paper, different-coloured pens and a mind-map are my way to work things through. I take one option and write words, phrases and questions in different colours as they occur to me and as they bounce off each other, creating new thoughts. I live in the 'world' of that choice and see what comes out.

You can also do it in a more physical way – by taking twenty-four hours and living as if you had made a certain decision. Let's assume you've got to decide between two distinct choices: to take a job in your nearest town or Paris. Live each of them for twenty-four hours and see how it feels. Whenever you go out, spend money, talk to friends, go to a meeting, plan a party, etc, you think about what that would be like for you if were about to start a new job in your local town. What would be different and the same? What would be better or worse? Notice how it feels to consider these new options and imagine these different scenarios.

Now live for twenty-four hours imaging that you are about to live in Paris and do the same reflecting. Does one choice come out on top? Or did your clever brain propose a shiny new option that you'd never thought of before?

You could also use pros/cons lists, mood boards or a good old chat with a friend or partner who will challenge and question you. Or a mixture of all of them! Whatever works for you, the main goal here is to give yourself the time to think in a rational and personal way.

It may sound like I'm very anti-spontaneity. You may be thinking: *This all sounds very calculated and boring and surely my gut instinct will guide me in an instant, won't it?* You're right of course, your 'gut instinct' will always have an opinion, which is driven by thousands of tiny signals you've picked up consciously and unconsciously about the decision you're making. There are plenty of times when you'll go with it with barely a second's pause and it will be perfect for you. Live for the moment!

The time for a more deliberate approach is when your helpful 'gut' is actually not being that helpful at all and appears to be equally happy for all options. That's when you need a back-up plan. It can also be a relief at times of major, life-altering decisions to have a way to explore your gut-instinct choice and run it through a few checks to see if it stacks up. It can stop the paralysis of indecision.

Of course, the ironic thing with all this talk of decision-making is that no choice is ever final anyway. It's exceptionally rare that an outcome will happen exactly the way you plan it in your head. We don't live in an isolated, sealed bubble. The thousands of influences on our life from people, nature, technology, laws, governments, our own health, you name it, will all have their own part to play in our future. We can only control so much and those unexpected intrusions into our plans will always provide us with excitement, opportunity, change and even more decisions.

So: pause, consider your options, make a decision and move forward. Any decision is better than no decision.

THRIVE: EXERCISE 2

This is an easy one! Pick one important decision that you must make in the near future, something that is playing on your mind at the moment. Then use one of the techniques above or a hybrid of your own making and work through the options.

How did it go? Was it easy or hard to explore all angles of the choices? Did something unexpected come up? Have you made the decision?

THRIVE: RELAX INTO YOUR OWN SKIN

Your friend's head pokes above the top of her boat, *'Left. I'm going left,'* she announces.

Oh. Your chest tightens. You hadn't realised how much you'd been hoping she'd make the same decision as you! You can still change your mind. You haven't said anything in response yet. Oh goodness, this is so hard! Left could be good for you too, couldn't it? But if you took it, then it would always be you agreeing with her decision rather than you following the course that you believed to be right for you. No, it has to be right.

'That sounds great, I'm sure it will give you some brilliant opportunities. I had decided to go right though, so I guess we'll be parting ways here.' As the words leave your mouth, your brain and your heart both give you a reassuring hug. You've got to stick to 'you'.

You spend the next few minutes chatting, laughing and saying your goodbyes. You part on good terms, sure that you'll bump into her again at some point in the future. She glides off into the left-hand channel, raising her hand in a final farewell.

Dwelling on this moment for too long will kick you into over-thinking mode and you'll start to consider following her, which deep-down you know isn't right for you. So, with nothing else to stop you, you surge forward and angle the boat to the right. Let's see where this takes you! We're ready! Your brain and your heart cry out in an unusual moment of agreement.

The current is fast but predictable and you now find it easy enough, although the speed certainly keeps you on your toes. You round the corner and spot a sight you haven't seen a while. Glimmering large and impressive is your palace. It's still a way off, but the details are becoming clearer and its size almost takes your breath away. When you had first glimpsed it at the start of this journey, you hadn't appreciated its sheer scale and beauty. It's comforting that you still feel confident and excited; this is still the place for you. You have come along way visit this great landmark and you've earned your entrance ticket.

Suddenly two smaller boats dive out of a side stream at top speed, right into your path. The whooping and shouts of adrenaline-fuelled joy make you smile even as you rush to haul your boat to one side to avoid a collision.

'Sorry mate, sorry, didn't see you there. Wow, that was incredible! We took a side stream a little way back, looking for a bit of adventure and to cut off this massive bend in the main river, y'know, gotta be done, right?! And we came across this intense patch of rapids which capsized me three times and almost broke the boat in two. Then, you'll never guess, it shot us over this waterfall, no warning at all, I tried to warn this other dude who followed me but he couldn't hear me over the sound of the water, so we both dived head-first down this huge drop off. Luckily this little beauty stayed upright and I landed hard but upright at the bottom. What a ride! Then, just as I was catching my breath, I got sucked into ANOTHER set of rapids just back there. Got chucked around a bit, I don't mind telling you, but I'm here, so I guess I did it right!' *The story floods out of him at top speed, while he breathes heavily, grinning from ear to ear.*

Your brain has a few thoughts about this guy: 'We've got a right one here: reckless, thoughtless and selfish. A cowboy flying by the seat of his pants who's lucky to be alive and with no respect for those around him or the power of the river. Let's leave him to it.' *As usual, your heart takes a different tack:* 'Well maybe he IS all those things, but he's also full of energy and joy. He seems to realise that he's here more by luck than judgement and he's just riding that luck until it runs out. He's an optimist."

As you can feel yourself still smiling and warming to this crazy character, you have to agree that his energy and sense of fun are infectious. He has clearly by-passed all the training rapids and doesn't bother with much reflection or learning, but he's getting out of it what he wanted. You admire his brash, simple goal of just having fun. He's obviously comfortable on his own, barely checking to see if the 'other dude' is still even afloat so he doesn't need anything from you. It could be fun to ride alongside him for a while, you could do with a good laugh at some crazy stories.

BE PROUD OF YOUR DECISIONS

When you've made an important decision, even if it feels right, it won't stop the little nagging feeling that maybe you should have chosen a different option. Just as in the boat, your friends or events around you could have you second-guessing yourself. You can acknowledge the feeling and use it as a helpful prompt to check the reasoning behind your decision, but don't let the actions or opinions of others carry too much weight in your decision.

You deserve to be where you are. You've worked hard, made the mistakes, taken the learnings and lived every moment. This is your life; be proud of it and trust yourself. There isn't another person alive who has exactly the same life as you, so no one can ever be completely in your shoes. Only you can make the decisions which are right for you. You are unique in every sense. This should give you strength and confidence, but it can feel also little lonely at times, so don't worry if this feeling creeps in too. Just like in our story, you'll never be alone for long!

HAVE FUN

This sounds so simple that you may be wondering why on earth I've bothered to make a point of it. It IS worth a mention though, mainly because if you let it, work can sap all the fun out of you. This isn't because work can't be fun but more down to your perception of what work should be.

Earlier in the book we talked about our internal negative and positive voices and how these can have a huge impact on your actions and emotions. If you're the sort of person who sings in the car when you're driving a colleague to a meeting or brings in chocolate-chip cookies on a Wednesday for the office to share 'just because', then you're already halfway there because you're looking for the fun in the 'everyday'.

It's true that fun is what you make it. It's also true that work won't be a day-long party, Monday to Friday. So, it's your responsibility to find the little things in your working environment which you enjoy ... and then make time to do them.

As you get more senior in your career, the common perception is that work gets more serious and less fun. My view on that is it doesn't have to. Yes, your responsibility increases. Yes, your decisions have bigger impacts. Yes, you'll have a lot on your plate. But all those things are still true whether you sing your heart out to your favourite song in the car or not, so you may as well take the opportunities for fun and enjoy them. I promise that no one else will hear your guilty pleasures playlist, so crank up the volume!

THRIVE: EXERCISE 3

★ When was the last time you remember having fun or a lighter moment at work?

★ What type of thing could you do to bring a little light relief to your office or job which others would appreciate too?

★ Make a list of all the things you've achieved – try to add things that you worked hard at or found challenging. Put it somewhere easy to find for those days when you need a little reassurance.

THRIVE: PASS IT FORWARD

Your new buddy is fun. You haven't laughed so much in ages. He's so willing to laugh at his own mistakes and it makes you realise that you've done some cringe-worthy but very funny stuff too. He's great company and brings a different energy to the journey.

You realise quickly that his adrenaline-fuelled shortcut has meant that he hasn't built up the skills to comfortably read and navigate through the ever-changing water course. He misses the signs, which means that new challenges take him by surprise and he's not prepared.

The first set of rapids that you encounter together ends with you dragging his boat out of a vicious spin which would have seen him capsize and be swept underwater in a matter of seconds. He's grateful but seemingly unaffected, shaking himself from top to bottom like a dog in an effort to rid himself of the cold sweat he'd felt in the heat of the moment. He then smiles and calmly turns his boat into the current once again, *'Oohh – that was a bit close, eh?!' and pushes off.*

Your brain is scathing and superior. "So it looks like Mr No-Care-In-The-World isn't quite as great as he thinks he is! We may both be in at the same point in the river at the moment, but it's clear who's having the most successful journey. He'd never have got out of that spin if we hadn't been there! He should be thanking us with every fibre of his being, begging to be taught how to do better!"

Your heart sadly listens in. "That's how it is now, is it? You want to be the hero? You want everyone to hang off your every word just because you helped out in a difficult situation? Sure, he isn't as experienced as you so he probably could learn a thing or two, but he's **here**, isn't he? He's at the same point as you. And looking like he's having more fun too! What does that tell you? I'm guessing that in spite of all his stories of mishap that actually he's pretty good at assessing risk. He's also found quicker and more direct ways to go. What could we learn from him?"

Your brain's ego shrinks a little bit and it goes quiet. Your heart has made a good point.

You notice that although your companion doesn't ask for help or advice, he's spending more time just behind your boat, watching your every move. He asks you for your story on how you got to where you are now and then listens attentively to the details of your adventures along the river and what you've learnt.

You realise that this guy learns by doing, so you make sure to comment on things as you navigate bends, shallow water and fast channels, just voicing what's going through your head, sharing your thought processes and decision-making tips. He says very little apart from the odd joke or sarcastic comment so you're not sure if he's taking anything in or not, but it's no effort for you and you find that you enjoy sharing your knowledge – even if it's just with the water.

The light catches the domed roof of your palace and you can see the deep green of the tiles come to life with shadows and ridges. More details are showing themselves every day as you get closer and closer, some are surprising and others comforting. You feel a ripple of excitement tinged with nerves run through your body.

A shout brings you out of your daydream. Your buddy is waving his arms. While your mind was elsewhere, he has pushed ahead and is a little front of you, now standing in his boat, desperately trying to get your attention. At first, you're not sure what he's so excited about, but then your ears home-in on the distinctive gurgle and rush of water at the edge of rapids.

Your brain switches into gear, while your heart quietly mutters, smiling, "He must have been paying attention to something you said because he spotted those rapids well before you!"

From what you can see, these rapids don't look too bad; certainly similar to ones you've managed in the past. You're fairly sure you'll be able to pass through them without much incident. There is another dimension now though, as you watch the boat ahead of you closely. You feel a sense of responsibility for your new friend. By sharing your knowledge with him, you suddenly realise that you're invested in how he manages these rapids. You really want him to put his new knowledge to the test and succeed. Now you're not only navigating your boat, but you've got half an eye on what he's doing, willing him to 'read' the river, see the subtle signs and react with skill and precision.

At the first torrent he misses the unnaturally smooth surface on a section of water in front of him and his bow hits the underwater rock that was causing it. He's thrown off his feet as the boat lurches to the side. You gasp loudly and power forwards to reach his boat as fast as you can and help. Your brain scolds you for thinking you were such a great teacher as disappointment and fear surge though your body.

You're within a few metres of him when his head pops up and without a glance in your direction, he skillfully takes control once again, manoeuvring away from the sunken danger and out into the main current. He's back and with a whoop of joy he quickly negotiates the next portion of river without any hint of uncertainty or fear. His natural bravery combined with his newly acquired skills are working well for him, but you can't help but feel some anger bubble inside you.

You're about to shout angrily at him, criticize his technique and warn him that if he carries on like this he'll get himself killed and put in danger anyone who tries to help him. Your lips form around a cry of, *'What on earth were you thinking? You shouldn't be on the river acting like that!'* when something stops you. You pause to at look at him. He's fine, better than fine, his skills are improving by the minute. Where was the anger really coming from?

You weren't in any real danger so are you perhaps a little jealous that he can be so carefree and 'live for the moment'?

You relax a little and ponder your own attitude.

It's interesting how quickly our brains can judge another person by comparing them to our own worldview. In the same way as your path has been special, so has everyone's. You only ever get to see a snapshot of someone else's journey and they of yours. It's fair to assume that they are equally as proud of their decisions and experiences as you are. So instead of making assumptions, try to use some empathy and switch into learning mode to see what you can learn from someone different from you; you never know what gems you could pick up.

Your knowledge and experience at this point will often be more extensive than some of those around you at work. Just as with the new guy on the river, you will likely be able to pick up on subtle hints that you've experienced more than them. This can give you a level of authority and you'll hopefully earn the respect of your colleagues by drawing on that deep well of information to help move things forwards. You'll find that people refer to you on certain topics and that you are invited into discussions to give your opinion. This can be a bit strange to start with and you may start to doubt yourself, but try to go back to the principle of **Know Yourself**. Give yourself a minute to think through all the experience and insights that you have which you could offer at that meeting. **Take responsibility** for your presence there and make sure that you are fully engaged and generous with your inputs. You deserve to be there.

The famous *Spiderman* quote also rings in my head at these times: *'With great power comes great responsibility.'*

Perhaps you don't consider your power to be that great – after all, when was the last time you dived off a high-rise building, in freefall, attached by a thread, to catch a falling person who was looking at a sticky end?! Perhaps your power is a little more mundane and human than that, but you still possess it, nonetheless. How to use it wisely and avoid abusing it, are skills that we don't all possess naturally, as can be seen by the all-too-frequent scandals involving high-profile, 'powerful' people who have wreaked havoc on those with whom they have come into contact. The #metoo movement started to show the extent to which this is unfortunately a reality for many.

Luckily, as you've got this far into the book, you've already got the toolkit to avoid becoming a power-hungry, insensitive, self-absorbed idiot! Just look to your Guiding Principles: **Take Responsibility, Show Empathy** and **Know Yourself.** Use these as a compass and you won't go too far wrong.

STAY CURIOUS

Passing on what you've learnt and helping others to learn from your experiences benefits you as much as them. As well as feeling helpful, useful and appreciated, there are two important factors to consider; you can learn from them and your own knowledge becomes deeper.

As within the story, we all get used to our way of doing things – it's only natural. But it is only one way to do it and we will always tend towards our strengths and rely on our education and habits to help guide us. As we've seen before, every single human is unique, which means that there is no one other person who would naturally follow exactly the way you do something. We can all conform to a convenient norm when we have to (although there is an argument about how much that helps anyone or any society if too many people start conforming too often) but as a rule, there will always be more than one way to do everything. The more curious you are about those other ways, the richer your life will become.

Imagine if you only ever ate cold food. You can be perfectly healthy and satisfied with cold food. No doubt you'd find your way around potentially awkward situations when hot food was being offered and your life would carry on without incident. However, by exploring hot food and talking to people who ate it, you would open up a whole new culture and with it, new traditions, vocabulary, social occasions and experiences. When was the last time you researched a completely new idea or subject? When did you last talk to someone about their religion or hobby? Stay curious.

Linked to this point is the value of questioning what you already know. Anyone who has ever had a conversation with a four-year-old will know that you can very quickly get yourself tied in knots trying to explain something you thought you knew like the back of your hand. The culprit of this frustrating mental dance isn't the four-year-old, it's the question 'Why?'. Imagine the conversation you might have with four-year-old Robbie:

Why are you singing to the radio?

Because I like this song.

Why?

Because it's got a tune I like and the words mean something to me.

Why don't you sing to all songs?

Ummm... Because they don't all have the same effect on me.

Why?

Well... ummmm... Because everyone reacts differently to music, a song that some people may love, others may find annoying.

Why do you sound like that when you sing? If you love something why aren't you better at it?

Ahem... well... I know my singing isn't the best but I enjoy it, it makes me feel good. I can lose myself for a minute in the words and music. It doesn't matter if I'm not very good at it, it's more about the feeling that singing gives me.

Oh. My favourite song is Old MacDonald. Can I have a biscuit?

Robbie gets a biscuit and toddles off, leaving you questioning what else could you do just for the feeling, without worrying whether or not you're any good at it. Has your fear of what others may think stopped you from doing things that you perhaps you could have loved? Why do we feel we have to be perfect at something to enjoy it? You Google 'amateur choir near me' and see what results pop up while Robbie finishes his biscuit, completely oblivious to the ripples he has just created in your mind.

By explaining your decisions and actions to someone and answering their 'whys?' you'll be forced to dig a little deeper into your habits and beliefs. Sometimes this will help to solidify them and other times this may lead you to question yourself. Either way, it's a good thing! Embrace the challenge.

There's always the obvious benefit of generosity too… You will find happiness in the happiness of others. Smiles are infectious. Seeing someone smile and enjoy a skill that you've taught them is addictive. It's such a small, easy thing to do – passing on something you're good at to someone else who's interested – and it can even rekindle your love for it at the same time. Sometimes the smallest gestures reap the biggest rewards. Be curious and generous.

TAKE BIG DECISIONS SLOWLY

At the start of your career, every decision you need to make can feel weighty, important and difficult. It can seem as though one wrong step could ruin all you've worked for. Generally speaking, this isn't the case, but decision-making is a skill to be honed. As you progress through your career, the number of decisions you need to make will get to such a volume that you'll be forced to sift them. Spotting the few important ones within the general sludge of the minor ones isn't always easy, but stick to the three Guiding Principles and give yourself some time and you'll find your own ways to prioritise.

Others will be relying on your decisions to keep things moving and to make significant changes, so you can't procrastinate about each one. Make the easy decisions fast and the big ones slowly.

GIVING AND TAKING CRITICISM

Criticism can be awkward and uncomfortable to give and receive, but it is also a fact of life and definitely a fact of career progression. The best way to make it work for you is to think about our three Guiding Principles again. Let's dive into some specifics.

Take Responsibility

Criticism can be a gift. It can hold nuggets of truth and open our eyes to seeing things in new ways. If we take responsibility, we can control our own response to it. As humans, we have the tendency to interpret, assume and add our own commentary to everything we see and hear, which can completely skew the original intention, if we're not careful. By asking ourselves one question before we react, we can save ourselves a lot of heartache.

Simply look at the exact words that were said to you and ask, 'How much of this is 100% true?' Try to be as objective as you can. If you can find the grain of truth, that is what holds the key to learning something useful and can turn a potentially negative situation into a more positive one. You may even end up thanking your criticiser!

If you get the chance, a great way to do this is to write down every thought about the criticism on some paper. Just write whatever is in your head and use SHOUTY CAPITALS if you need to. Get it all out and keep writing as your train of thought helps you to unpick it. This can be a great way of uncovering some truths that may have been hidden initially.

Show Empathy

Once again, it's about trying to give yourself a little distance from the personal nature of the criticism and judging the position of the person giving it. Do you know everything about this person? Why have they decided to criticise you? What impact has your action possibly had on them? Are there other factors which are influencing their thoughts?

Know Yourself

Know yourself well enough to find the truth within the criticism, understand the implications and decide if it's something that you believe you need to work on. When criticism makes a direct hit and makes us feel raw or exposed, this is when you can immediately feel that there is some truth in it. Although it can be hard to face at times, if you focus on this truth, it can give you a clear path for self-improvement. Remember, though, that everyone thinks differently, so you may not agree that your actions are worthy of criticism. Decide a course of action and move on. Don't wallow or keep obsessing about criticism; use it and learn or disregard it and move on.

Giving criticism

True criticism, however awkward it feels, can be liberating because it shines a clear light on an area we need to work on. Damaging criticism is quite the reverse and at this point of your career journey you will likely be managing people or working as part of a close team. This is why you need to be very careful about how you deliver criticism. This is when the comment made has a tiny element of truth to it but it has been taken out of context or misunderstood, which means that it is plausible enough that the receiver struggles to deny it outright. This leads to a feeling of complete powerlessness. The person will shrink back and retreat, unable to find a way to fight back. This sort of behaviour sows seeds of resentment and frustration which can fester over time.

The relationship between you as a manager or leader and the rest of your team will only **thrive** if there is trust that runs both ways. Particularly if you have responsibility for more junior people: they trust you to help guide their career, interpret the working world around them and bolster their talent.

You hold your team in the palm of your hands. They are vulnerable because as someone who works very closely with them, you see everything they do (and don't do), how they act and which things affect them. It is precisely because you see everything that you could potentially have a lot of critical 'material' if you scrutinized each of their actions. Your job is to carefully choose what to highlight and have clear reasons why. You need to sift through the weeds and decide which area you want to nurture.

Remember that whatever you choose needs to be 100% true to avoid falling into the trap of damaging criticism. It also needs to be true for THEM, not for you! When other people's actions trigger a negative reaction within you, that is YOUR issue to work on, not theirs. It's too easy to hide our own frustrations and weaknesses behind a blast of criticism directed at someone else; that's called redirection and avoidance.

There is a real risk that criticism which isn't well-chosen and managed could end up blocking, stifling or severely disrupting someone's career. It's always worthwhile taking the time to work through any constructive feedback that you feel you need to give to someone. Check all the angles: the validity, the impact, the frequency, the dependencies and the history.

Your only goal when giving criticism is to show someone how to improve and explain why it is important. Make sure is it framed correctly, with the right perspective and balance. The person should see this as useful information which they can actively use for self-improvement and growth. You can even state this in your conversation with them, to make sure for you and for them, that you have a clear reason for discussing it.

You can say something like, *"I have noticed the last three times that XXXX has happened, you have reacted XXXX. I'm bringing this up because I'm not sure if you're aware of the impact this is having on XXXX. I'm looking out for you and we can easily work on a solution together so that this doesn't escalate into anything more serious. Have you noticed this happening? What prompts you to react in this way?*

Our three Guiding Principles in this instance are clear:

★ **Take responsibility** for the whole situation when you see the need to give criticism.

★ **Show empathy** every step of the way to ensure that you're not doing more harm than good.

★ **Know yourself** by not letting your own issues

cloud your judgement or get in the way.

The best managers nurture, support and encourage their teams. This doesn't mean avoiding criticism; it means maintaining that bond of trust by being strategic, careful and always truthful.

THRIVE: EXERCISE 5

★ How are you generous with your knowledge and skills?

★ Can you remember when you last gave up some time to teach something or help someone out?

★ Try being the curious toddler and asking, 'But why?' the next time you're in a new situation or when a question occurs to you. Keep digging until you fully understand.

★ Write down an occasion when you have received damaging criticism. Flesh out all the details about what happened, what was said, how you felt about the criticism and about the person giving it and what happened after. Now do the same for a more positive experience of receiving criticism. How did it differ? What can you learn from both approaches? What will you take forward into your next conversation when you need to be critical?

As we've been delving a little deeper into our own motivations and behaviours, it would seem like a good point to investigate our final Guiding Principle with a Deep Dive into Knowing Yourself.

GUIDING PRINCIPLES DEEP DIVE 3: KNOW YOURSELF

This is an area I admit to struggling with for many years. People would ask me what I wanted to do in my career and I'd just shrug and say, 'I'm not sure'. Then daily life picked up pace and my decisions would just get made, usually by taking the easiest options.

I'm lucky that more often than not, these were good solid decisions and I did have enough insight to push for something else when I needed to. I have also worked with some wonderful people who have looked out for me even when I wasn't really doing it for myself. These people are like gold dust, but they won't always be there. Their help should be a blessing, not a strategy.

But looking back, I think I rarely checked in with myself to review if a decision I was making was something that really played to my strengths and ambitions. As a result, I got to forty and realised that although I was very successful in my career – steadily progressing from entry level into management and eventually to heading up an international function – there was something missing. There was a hole that I couldn't figure out how to fill. I was happy but not satisfied.

The reason I couldn't plug the gap (and no one else could do it for me either) was because I had lost track of the things that made me tick. What did I love to do as a child? What were my natural strengths? Where had I really excelled at work and enjoyed it? What made me smile? What made me feel invigorated and ready to conquer the world?

How could I possibly take my career by the horns and surge forward if I didn't know why I was doing it or what I was aiming for?

There are a hundred books, podcasts and TED talks on how to find your 'true self' or your 'spirit' or your 'passions' so I'm not going to rehash those here, but throughout your career journey it's a great idea to check-in with yourself on a regular basis to get a sense of how well-connected you are to your inner 'you' and how closely your external life reflects your inner world.

When working with my mentees I find it really important to spend some time on this at the start of our relationship so that I can understand their motivations and drivers. This makes it easier to notice when something they are proposing to do doesn't sit right or when they are struggling to make a decision, I can guide them back to their purpose.

Here are some easy exercises to kick things off:

THRIVE: EXERCISE 6

1. Spend some time exploring what makes you tick.
We're looking here for things that evoke strong emotions, both good and bad.

I'd suggest you try to end up with a few different lists:

★ What activities light me up? What makes me excited to think of doing it? What will I make extra efforts to do? Equally, what do I naturally recoil from? What do I avoid doing at all costs?

★ What qualities do I have that I'm really proud of or that come easily? What do people say I'm very good at or why would someone want to be my friend/get to know me?

★ What are my priorities in life?

★ What have I always wanted to try? If I had no fear, anxiety or limitations, what would I do?

The aim of these lists is to unearth the 'you' without boundaries or fears or the restrictions of social conventions. It can be really liberating to find even one thing on the list that you could actually do or at least start to make steps towards doing.

An example could be: You love nurturing/playing with young family members/teaching people and seeing them grow. This doesn't mean that you have to throw in your job in engineering to become a teacher, it just means that perhaps you can look at how you can be a mentor to graduates coming into the business or research any local schools that you could get involved with. Try to be as open and honest in your lists as possible, really dive into your past, your personality and how you'd like to be in the future.

2. Explore what your triggers are for negative emotions:

★ What makes you stressed and angry and upset?

★ Are you more likely to deal with a problem internally and worry about it or react openly and quickly?

★ What are your coping strategies for when things go wrong?

★ How does your body feel when you're in a negative place?

Sometimes it's not the obvious answer. For example, you have no particular feelings about dishwashers, so why do you always feel your anger rise when you see that it has been stacked wrongly and therefore won't wash the plates properly? This is much more likely to be about the level of control that you feel you need in situations and your low tolerance for (needless) repetition of tasks, rather than an issue over a few dirty plates. You'll probably find that you've reacted in a similar way about something at work which had comparable triggers.

Nothing of what you find out about yourself is bad. It's important to remember this. This exercise isn't intended to show you your faults and highlight how awful you (think) you are! The point is awareness. You can't control or improve something that you aren't aware of. Awareness can also help you prevent the reaction in the first place and help you feel more in control of a situation.

3. The Five Whys.
This is a version of the 'why' conversation that we had with little Robbie a few pages back. Write down what you do for a job or want to do for a job and why you like it. Then look at that sentence and ask, 'Why?' and write down the answer. Then take that sentence and ask 'Why' again. Try to keep going for at least five 'Whys'. Your answer should move closer and closer to your core beliefs, passions or desires.

Here's an example using my job:

I am a coach and mentor and I like it because I get value from supporting people.

WHY?
Because I have experience and knowledge that I think can help them.

WHY?
Because previous experience has shown me that I'm good at getting to know individuals and helping them to open up and that's when I can really make a difference.

WHY?
Because connecting with others and seeing my input help someone is very rewarding for me.

WHY?
Because I want to feel that my uniqueness has value beyond shaping me.

WHY?
Because helping everyone recognise and value their uniqueness is my superpower.

This leads me to a new statement about me and my job, instead of the old one which was:
I am a coach and mentor and I like it because I get value from supporting people.

I now have:
I am a coach and mentor and I like it because helping everyone

recognise and value their uniqueness is my superpower.

Which do you feel has more power and authenticity?

4. Look at psychometric tools to help you understand yourself and others.
A method such as the **Insights** Discovery process analyses your preferences, style and strengths in relation to a work environment and how you interact with others with different styles. This particular one is a psychometric tool based on the psychology of Carl Jung. It uses a simple and memorable four-colour model, called the colour energies, to help people understand their style, their strengths and the value they bring to the team. Everyone is a unique mix of Fiery Red, Sunshine Yellow, Earth Green and Cool Blue energies, which determines how and why people behave the way they do. They can be very revealing and help you understand why you behave the way you do around certain people and in certain situations. It's most effective when a whole team or department or even company can do it.

Knowing yourself will also help you to stand out, without necessarily needing to be the loudest, shiniest, most 'in your face' person in the room. By using your strengths and producing excellent work, you'll stand out on your own merit. Being average and lack-lustre with your work is the easiest way to lie back in your boat and surrender control to the current, letting yourself drift.

The bigger the organisation, the more important it is to stand and be seen for the right reasons at the right times by the right people. People in your business need to know who you are and what you

stand for if they are going to bring you to the table ...
and you need to be sure of that too!

THRIVE: ENJOY YOUR DESTINATION ... OR LEARN WHY YOU NEVER ARRIVED.

Over the last few miles you've been creeping nearer and nearer to the palace and now it's within touching distance. You've made it.

You've been talking about this place to your companion and had vaguely assumed that as he was in the same place as you, that he would be heading to the same destination. Well, you got that one wrong – a quick note to never assume anything, pings in your brain!

He listens very politely to you talk about the palace and then comments that it sounds a bit too grand and permanent for him. He's much happier taking chances on the smaller rivers, seeking out adventure and generally flying by the seat of his pants. He understands that you need to arrive on your own and in your own time, so with a cheery wave and a *'See ya!'* he forks off down another smaller channel and is gone.

Slowly now, your brain and your heart quiet and focused, you approach the palace. Fear and excitement bubble in your stomach. You can't take your eyes off it. From the glimpses you've been getting along your journey you already had a good picture of what it would look like, but now you can feel its energy. You know you're ready to enter and now impatience to see inside takes over and you surge forward.

As the river glides to the wide entrance, you notice that there's a dock to moor the boat on the left but then the river carries on around the side and disappears off once again into the distance. Your heart whispers, *'Oohh I wonder what's out there?'*

'We've only just got here,' chides your brain. *'Let's see what this place is like first, shall we?'*

Once inside, you run around the palace in excitement, like a child at a playground, trying things for a few moments and then moving on. You start to see the areas that are familiar and those that will require further investigation. Your over-riding emotion is pleasure. Thank goodness! It was all worth it.

You can stay in your palace as long as you choose, understanding that the river that curls around its foundations is never going away. You invite people to visit; some stay a while and some are only brief meetings. There are days when you feel that you can't ever feel comfortable in this huge place, but then other days when you feel like it was built just for you. One day you know you'll feet will itch to be back in the boat again, exploring what the river has to offer further downstream, but for now, you sit back and enjoy your success.

Well done! You've become the future career persona that you created at the start. While nothing that we ever imagine is 100% right or perfect, hopefully you find enough of what you were looking for to feel content and successful.

It can often be the case that as you get closer, you assume that others around you also want that same goal. Perhaps they do and perhaps they don't. Before you start to get defensive and jealous it's always worth checking your assumptions to avoid wasting any energy on needless exhausting emotions. If other people do want the same as you, then having to fight a bit harder for it at the last moment can help crystallise in your mind how much you want it and you may need to think of an unusual or innovative way to make your final play. Just don't give up!

Once you've arrived, after the initial relief of getting there, it's totally normal to have a quick look around, see all the dark corners and hidden rooms and think, 'Uh oh, what have I done?!' No one can possibly know everything about a new situation, however much they research and prepare. Ask anyone who moves into a house advertised as *'fully updated and ready to move in, no work needed'* and see how long it takes them to make a 'work to do' list.

Just try not to freak yourself out with all the stuff that you don't understand. There's always a massive learning curve in any new situation. That's also part of why you wanted to get here, remember? For the new challenges and to push your comfort zones. When the inevitable 'freak-out' does happen though, just remember two things:

1. You deserve you be there. Try to look at yourself the way someone else does: you worked hard, learnt the skills, built the relationships... You earned your place. You've been in difficult situations before and got through it. You've got this! Trust yourself.

2. There's plenty you DO know. There's no shame in retreating into your comfort zone of something you do understand while you figure out the new stuff. You will naturally focus on what you can't do and it's easy to forget just how much you **can** do. Give yourself a little time and perspective and figure out who can help you.

Although in our story you reach your palace, you're smart enough to realise that sometimes things don't go the way you planned. Perhaps someone else has got there first or a totally unforeseen event has closed the palace (for a real-life example, consider the enormous impact COVID-19 had on our lives). In these instances, give yourself some breathing space and go back to your three Guiding Principles:

Take Responsibility: Be gracious in defeat. Try to learn why you didn't succeed, is there something you were missing? What would you do differently if you had another stab at it?

Show Empathy: Consider who got there instead... Can you see the logic behind their success or the impossible choices that someone had to make? Be happy for their success. You can easily imagine the amount of effort that someone else had to put in to be at the same point as you; they deserve it too. Also, if you know the person, they may well be feeling guilt at upsetting their colleague and friend, so reassure them. Focus instead on being grateful for the lessons you've learnt and the skills you've honed on the journey.

Know Yourself: Let yourself feel the disappointment. Explore what exactly it is about not achieving your goal that leaves you upset and frustrated. Are there other feelings now bubbling up once the initial adrenaline has passed? Perhaps some relief, feeling lost, even betrayal if you believed that it was a 'done deal'. It's so important to acknowledge those feelings and give yourself time to work through them and understand them, as they will give you fuel for what you do next. Just don't get stuck with them for too long as they can suck you down like quicksand and make you lose sight of the bigger picture.

Going back into yourself and re-evaluating your values, your dreams, your life situation and your passions will help to give you focus on how to move forward. It may be that you want to hang around and have another go at the same goal, once you've looked at how you could improve. Or perhaps the event has changed your outlook and you feel that you need to move in a different direction. The point is that our river story doesn't end and it doesn't go in circles, it just keeps moving forwards, always flowing.

There may be times when you find yourself returning to the ADAPT phase, with a new goal in sight. Whenever we start from a new place, the journey onwards will be exciting and challenging all over again, but in a different way, because you've got so much more to draw on this time. You'll find a new river with a new palace and some of the views and obstacles will be familiar and some will be fresh out of the box – that's what keeps things interesting!

The great news is that you can't get this wrong! There's no one right answer. Life is all about these moments. As I said at the start of the THRIVE stage, our career is about the whole journey, there is no end-point or final goal, just stops along the way. So, appreciate every situation for what it is and move on to your next adventure.

THRIVE: EXERCISE 7

★ Write down what you remember about the last time you succeeded in something.

★ How did it feel? What did you do? What impact did it have on your next move?

★ Now do the same again with a situation which didn't go as you expected.

★ Did anything unexpected come up? Do you feel more strongly about the success or the apparent failure?

OBSTACLES ALONG THE WAY

As we've seen, challenges are a part of life and an important part of our career journey too. They help us adapt, question our logic and grow a little wiser. There are some obstacles which will probably only make themselves known as you get into the THRIVE stage of your career. It is not that they didn't exist before, but now you are in a position where you can do something about them, so you pay more close attention to them. As you'll see, some of the obstacles are bigger than us as individuals, as they are routed deep in society, so your ability to make an impact will vary. However, awareness and understanding are the first step, then how you choose to respond will be up to you.

A NOT-SO-HEALTHY CAREER

My hope is that by following the guidance and the exercises in the book that you will have a good grip on understanding your body and the signals it gives you. With the best will in the world, however, daily life is loud and our body can't always make itself heard or we don't prioritise the time to reset and nip any issues in the bud. It's worth spending a little time considering what happens when we hit the snooze button on our body's nagging voice a few too many times. In short, we get ill and the longer we ignore the signs, the worse we get. Let's take a look at some of the main health-related career obstacles:

BURN-OUT

Burn-out is a real thing. It has been acknowledged by the World Health Organisation and the NHS (National Health Service in the UK). We can think of it as a condition resulting from chronic workplace stress that has not been successfully managed. Chronic means that the symptoms have been ongoing for a long while with little improvement. We're not just talking one bad day, we're talking months of persistent stress resulting in:

★ Feeling exhausted or low energy most of the time.

★ Feeling distanced, negative or apathetic about your job.

★ Reduced ability to get things done at work.

There are some big numbers around the impact of this syndrome on the healthcare system and even mortality rates. A team of Stanford researchers looked into how workplace stress affects health costs and mortality in the United States. They found that it led to spending of nearly $190 billion and nearly 120,000 deaths each year. The World Health Organization has done a recent study showing that depression and anxiety affect 615 million worldwide and cost the global workforce an estimated $1 trillion in lost productivity each year.

In short, it's serious and widespread. *The Harvard Business Review* has written about the increasing pressure on employers to do something at a business level by developing strategies and policies which minimise the causes and treat the early signs. This is a really positive step forward, but let's be honest, you are the best judge of how you feel stress and how you deal with pressure. Let's see if you can develop the tools to help yourself. No one wants to burn-out.

The scientific community has broadly agreed on some of the effects of burn-out as:

★ Excessive stress

★ Fatigue

★ Insomnia

★ Sadness, anger or irritability

★ Alcohol or substance misuse

★ Heart disease

★ High blood pressure

★ Type 2 diabetes

★ Vulnerability to illnesses

By knowing yourself, understanding your triggers and giving yourself time and space to reflect you can spot the signs early. Some of factors to watch out for are:

★ You have a heavy workload and work long hours.

★ You struggle with work-life balance.

★ You work in a helping profession, such as health care.

★ You feel you have little or no control over your work.

By using the exercises suggested as we've moved through this book, the aim is that you can establish the positive routines and behaviours which should flag any creeping burn-out issues before they grab hold of you.

IMPOSTER SYNDROME

You can think of Imposter Syndrome as the feeling of being inadequate and unprepared for the job in front of you. You feel like a fraud and are full of self-doubt, even in spite of any evidence that you are wholly capable. These feeling affects all areas of your life. You withdraw and grind to a stop.

The thoughts that someone with Imposter Syndrome may have are:

★ 'I must not fail.'

★ 'I feel like a fake.'

★ 'It's all down to luck.'

★ 'Success is no big deal.'

You may be thinking that everyone feels like this from time to time, particularly in a new job or when starting a new project. You're right. Academic research carried out on over 14,000 people in the US on Imposter Syndrome in 2020 showed that up to 82% of them showed signs of it. The real issue comes when it starts to affect your day-to-day life at work and it doesn't go away.

Those with Imposter Syndrome struggle to deliver their work; they hold themselves back, constantly self-criticise and feel inadequate, all of which leads to anxiety, depression, frustration, shame and low self-confidence.

Although Imposter Syndrome has many studies, academic research and 'real life' evidence to support its existence, it isn't yet recognised by the medical profession as a mental-health disorder.

As with Burn-Out, awareness and early prevention are your best weapons against the worst impacts of Imposter Syndrome.

SUPERWOMAN SYNDROME

I realise that this title may see anyone who doesn't identify as a woman instantly turning the page. While I understand your reaction, hang on for little longer. It's helpful for everyone to be aware of this lesser-known issue so that you can spot it in those around you and lend a hand.

The term 'Superwoman Syndrome' was first coined in 1984 by Marjorie Hansen Shaevitz in her book by the same name. It is exactly what is says it is: trying to be Superwoman. These are women who feel pressured to be able to do it all and they work hard to fill multiple roles. They are trying to juggle, family, career and social activities. This leads to overwork, overwhelm and over commitment and often exhaustion, anxiousness and stress.

According to an academic study in the US, these 'Superwomen' feel that they:

★ Must show strength

★ Must suppress their emotions

★ Must resist any show of vulnerability or dependence on anyone else

★ Must show a determination to succeed, even in the face of roadblocks

★ Must help others

These feelings are exacerbated when someone feels that they are the 'only one' in their team/ organisation/workplace. From my personal experience I think this could be extended to feeling like you're the 'only one' in social and family settings too; the only one who remembers the birthdays, the only one who arranges the nights out, the only one who knows which bin goes out when ... you get the picture. They noted that if these people said or did the wrong thing, stereotypes would get reinforced, or prejudices confirmed. For women, being an 'only' in the workplace is very common.

A research organisation, McKinsey confirms from their data:

'Twenty percent of the women in our latest Women in the Workplace report said they were commonly the only person of their gender in the room or one of very few. The figure is far higher in some sectors such as technology and engineering. For women of color, that number rose to 45 percent. For men, it was just 7 percent.'

This gender disparity is a whole conversation in itself, but in relation to Superwoman Syndrome it means that when women see that they are an 'only one' or very under-represented in a business, they then feel huge pressure to take on more, refuse help and ignore their emotions just to be taken seriously.

Some of the tips we covered earlier in the book help in the fight against Superwoman Syndrome, such as learning to say 'no', building a support network and delegating.

THE 5-G WORKFORCE CHALLENGES

Multi-generational working certainly has its challenges and as we will probably all work in 5-G environments (five generations all in the same workplace) at some point, we will likely witness the tension, frustration and sometimes outright anger that can build up! These generational gaps normally come up because of misunderstandings and an ignorance about the work and social expectations and preferences of the other generations. Those who are new to a business or at the starting point of their career can be seen as being the inexperienced ones, and therefore should just do what they're told and toe the line. The older generation can feel out of touch and threatened by rapidly changing technologies and cultures. Often the stereotypes kick in before we have chance to see the person behind them.

These are the age groups we're looking at:

★ Generation Z (1997–2012)

★ Millennials (1981–1996)

★ Generation X (1965–1980)

★ Baby Boomers (1946–1964)

★ Silent Generation (born between 1928 and 1945)

Each generation grows up in a different context and, as a result, their worldview, skill sets and expectations can vary dramatically. For instance, members of the Silent Generation are typically seen as being very conservative with money, while Baby Boomers are a bit more spend-happy. Gen Zers and Millennials are heavily tech-reliant and comfortable using social-media platforms, while older generations may prefer other forms of communication and ways of working. This generational meeting point is unlike any other social situation that we have in our lives in terms of power dynamics and politics, but it's not going away any time soon, especially as everyone is working to later in life. The best approach for dealing with it is awareness and empathy … and sometimes just to plain ignore it and walk away!

I've witnessed how damaging this intolerance can be, seeing people ignored, cut across or even told to stop talking in meetings because of outdated and preconceived notions of 'place' and authority. I know how humiliating and defeating it can feel for that person and if you get into a situation like this that is really affecting you, then talk to someone else (ideally who was also there) and get another point of view. I'll put money on the fact that they felt uncomfortable with this behaviour too and would never approve of treating someone in that way. Luckily these situations are happening less and less as business culture changes and catches up, but it's still something I'm sure you'll encounter at some point.

WOMEN AT WORK ... FOR THE MEN TOO!

I wish I didn't need to write this section. I wish gender didn't drive decisions and behaviours. I'm hopeful that over the next decade it will become like smoking at your desk: unbelievable that it ever happened. But for now, we are still in a situation where being a woman or showing 'female traits' is a disadvantage in most workplaces to some degree. That second point about female traits is important because it directly affects men too. This is a gender bias, not a biological sex bias.

It's important to start by broadening out the topic to discrimination as a whole, because we need to appreciate the bigger picture before considering the detail.

As humans, it's completely normal that we gravitate towards people who seem familiar to us. We join together and get a sense of belonging because we all share a trait that the group deems to be important, be that an ability to dance or a belief in a certain god. I'm sure you'll have heard people talk about 'my tribe' or being 'part of a tribe'. When you're within that tribe, you have certain privileges, like the right to speak, the right to be listened to, the right to be treated fairly and the right to work together with other members as equals. So far so normal. The challenging part comes when someone who isn't an accepted part of the tribe tries to join in and contribute or change things. The reaction we often see (and often have ourselves) is that they are made to feel 'less' in some way because they don't have the 'thing' that binds everyone else together. They may have other wonderful qualities to add to the tribe, but sometimes 'not having the thing' is too big a hurdle for the other members to overcome. Welcome to discrimination.

We all accept this notion of belonging to groups as part of our culture and even that certain groups demand and are granted more power, because of their size, history or demographics. Our acceptance of the 'need' for inequality between these groups is part of our culture too – someone has to be on top, has to have the power ... right?

Perhaps they do, but does just the act of belonging to a certain group automatically give a person or group of people the right to use their privilege to exclude, patronise, control and ignore other groups? Arguments about this run very deep and it's thanks to free speech in today's climate that we can confront, discuss and address the questions of fairness, equality and the use of privilege and power.

The patriarchal society in the Western world has for generations promoted and enforced the rules of its tribe (where the only rule of entry was to have a penis) which were taken as the superior model for reasons that only history can defend. This has led to an often sexist, racist, discriminatory way of life for a large percentage of people (the other fifty per cent of the population for starters). While it's true that many tribes exist, bonding people together in thousands of ways, exclusion from a certain tribe only becomes a real issue when it affects your ability to live your life as you see fit. If enough people are prevented from living a full life because of the rules of one group of people, it's no surprise that we start to see rebellion, hate, mistrust, anger, disapproval, fear and active sabotage against those rules gather pace.

I am acutely aware that as a white, educated, British-born woman I can never truly appreciate the hardships faced by many in our society, but I am aware that they exist and that means that I can't be silent about them. I am female and therefore part of one of the largest groups who are treated differently: that of the non-male gender. If by adding my voice to this and any other of these categories it can help us be heard and if by being conscious of my own behaviour and modelling that to my children, I can help things change – then that's what I'll do.

My views come from the central idea of uniqueness. I think we can all agree without any debate that we are unique and our lives are unique. This uniqueness means that we all view the world in a very slightly different way. It's incredible that two people can ever agree on anything, let alone groups of people or companies or institutions or countries or religions! It's for this reason that empathy is the only possible way forward.

We can never truly see the world through the eyes of another as there are just too many variables, but to appreciate that every single thing you believe can be interpreted differently, suddenly gives you an appreciation of the vast diversity of the human race. It's this empathy that I'm going to call on when we discuss women at work, because these aren't just issues facing women, but anyone whose lives are touched by women. If that includes you, then try to open your eyes and your heart to the many small and large prejudices that women encounter every day and make a personal vow to confront those which are within your power and change them. If everyone did their bit to eradicate prejudice within their own sphere, then the cumulative effect would be world changing.

HOW WE GOT HERE

The study in 2020 in France by NEOMA business school joins the long list of research papers demonstrating that companies that have women on the board who feel empowered in their positions perform better. They discovered having more women in these senior roles leads to less excessive risk-taking, greater efficiency and less 'managing' of the finances to try to show a position which may not be fully accurate.

Great! Easy to fix then... Simply hire more women to the board! Job done, let's all go home and pat ourselves on the back. Wait a minute, though, this brilliant new strategy for combatting female inequality on boards assumes two things: firstly, that there is a glut of suitable women just waiting by the door to be let in and secondly, that everyone on the board also wants this change. Let's look at the first one and to do that we need to consider a potted history of women at work.

LEGAL LANDSCAPE

In the UK, the Equal Pay Act 1970 and Sex Discrimination Act 1975 were turning points in equality. They meant that a woman could no longer be paid less than her male counterparts for equal work and she could no longer be sacked for taking maternity leave. She could also have a credit card without a male guarantor and be served equally at wine bars.

Bearing in mind the significance of these laws and rights (including the wine bar one!) remember that they only came into force fifty years ago. Putting some figures around this gives us some perspective: this means that around 25 million people in the UK in 2021 were born when these laws didn't exist and of that number, around 14 million are of working age (50-65). That's 14 million people that are in workplaces today who grew up in a time (or at least in a culture) where having a baby could legitimately lead to a woman losing her job. That's incredibly significant. Fifty years is a very short time frame since such radical change. These 50–65-year-olds may very well be in senior positions today and yet they started their working life when discrimination was commonplace and never questioned.

Cultural change does not happen the moment a law is passed, it takes many years, often more than a generation. So, the women and men who are in their fifties and older today grew up in a country that was built around belonging to the male tribe, where male domination and superiority were legal and encouraged. Not only does that affect the men's view of women in the workplace, but it also affects the women's view of themselves and what they are capable of.

This leads us into the reason why there ISN'T a glut of women hammering down the board room door just waiting to be let in.

CULTURAL IMPLICATIONS

In the decades following this new legal landscape, the women who did have the ambition and resilience to try to break through into senior roles found themselves in a highly male-dominated (often exclusively male) world. Success was very tightly defined by individual gain, salary, status and power and the winners showed traits such as assertiveness, competitiveness, independence, influence, control and problem-focused strategies.

Eagley and Johannesen-Schmidt carried out some interesting research in the USA in the early 2000s on the leadership styles of men and women. They investigated the disparity between the natural management style of women and the style demanded of senior leaders, which is more focused on masculine traits. The women then had two choices if they wanted to take director-level roles: they either changed to mirror these male behaviours or melted into the background, as their female traits were viewed as weak and not 'authoritative' enough. Those who took the first path were courageous, unapologetic trailblazers, who shocked the male corporate world with their confidence and strength. They did all women a huge favour in rocking the stereotypes and cracking that glass ceiling.

Unfortunately, although this started to get women into the top seats, they were women behaving as men. These women could not show any female traits for fear of seeming weak. Collaboration and consensus with others were seen as uncertainty; empathy and concern were seen time-wasting and listening to gather ideas and options was viewed as not 'knowing-your-stuff'. It's no surprise that many of these women got to their top jobs only to find that they were unhappy, unfulfilled and exhausted. It's takes energy to fight your instincts! We can see here the background behind the rise in workplace stress, imposter syndrome and burn-out.

It is true that we made huge strides through

those decades in the equality and recognition of the value of women in high-level jobs, but we had created a whole new problem in which women had to be pseudo-men to succeed. Men were equally being disadvantaged by these attitudes because any show of behaviour which was not classed as 'male' was labelled weak, so men found themselves in a macho-male straitjacket. Much of this behaviour still continues today and I have witnessed it many times myself.

To compound this, these same women were often still taking the roles at home of mother, partner, cleaner, chef, problem-solver and general domestic goddess. Here come the creeping tendrils of Superwoman Syndrome we looked at in the earlier part of this chapter – feeling like you need to do everything, perfectly, on-time and better than anyone else. It's no surprise that these women feel tired out and confused. Trying to have everything and be everyone isn't sustainable.

The ironic thing is that often the pressure to act this way comes from the women themselves –they have found themselves in this mid-point of cultural change, where they can't quite let go of all the old stereotypes, but they've glimpsed the possibilities of a future where women can have the power, influence and jobs they've always dreamed of.

This isn't the future I want for our young women of today. I want to show you the mistakes as well as the accomplishments. The professionals of today owe it to each other to truly welcome equity and diversity in all areas of their lives. Setting their expectations and finding their balance based on their own skills and desires, not by following the expectations of a culture and a corporate system which are still trying to catch up to them.

UNCONSCIOUS BIAS AND THE AUTHORITY GAP

The second part of the boardroom conundrum was to assume that everyone else on that board wanted more women to be part of it. Unfortunately, this just isn't the case. Let's put overtly sexist behaviour to one side for a second to consider the darker, more serious issue of unconscious bias.

Unconscious bias refers to the attitudes and stereotypes that we all hold, deeply engrained in our psyche and outside of our conscious awareness and control. We take visual, verbal and behavioural clues to categorise other people, by age, gender, ethnicity, social background, sexual orientation or education. These clues can be incredibly useful as we make our way through life. From a basic human survival standpoint our unconscious judgements or biases are necessary and essential. They help us to decide whether someone might be friendly or hostile. This process of rapid categorisation was suggested by the psychologist Joseph LeDoux to be an unconscious danger detector.

This ability to categorise also comes in handy in social situations. It allows us to understand the appropriate behaviours and expectations in any given setting. These 'rules' are stored within our unconscious and allow us to behave in socially acceptable ways and make everyday judgements without us actively being aware of doing so.

Prejudice and discrimination come when our brain starts to categorise for social labelling rather than for survival. In a work setting this can come from the way a person dresses, an accent, a visual identity (race, gender) or from the contents of a CV.

The authority gap comes from this unconscious bias. It's a phrase developed by Mary Ann Sieghart in her work exploring the challenges faced by powerful women when demonstrating authority. In a nutshell, it's the scenario whereby, despite being the most influential and accomplished person in the room, a woman will find herself belittled or presumed to be ignorant by the men around her simply because of her gender. If a man were to say the exact same thing it would be automatically granted more authority than when a woman of equal standing says it. Sieghart presents significant evidence that this exists in the highest echelons of our society, most notably within politics and influential governing bodies.

The unconscious bias held by men (and women) in our society expects women to be likeable, much more so than men. A women can do anything that man can do, but she must remain likeable. This gives women two options in these settings:

1: Be demure and quiet. This will lead her to be liked but not listened to.

2: Be confident and speak her mind: this will make others listen to her, but she won't be liked.

Overall, we don't like women to behave as confidently as men, we find it unlikeable, unrelatable and off-putting, but the only way to get listened to and taken seriously is by displaying male characteristics. So, if female traits aren't regarded as authoritative, what choice does a woman in power have?

Sieghart spoke at length to influential, pioneering women such as Hillary Clinton, Baroness Hale, Mary Beard and Mary McAleese about their struggles because of the authority gap. Even when they were the most influential person in the room, they found themselves being ignored, talked over, patronised and made to wait while their husbands were addressed first. When the men were challenged about their behaviour, the response was often, 'I was joking' or 'I didn't mean that.'

Our cultural bias against women in power is so ingrained and so unconscious that behaviours will only start to change when we are forced to confront our prejudices and bring them into our conscious mind. This is uncomfortable work and no one likes to be challenged on their automatic reactions, because we feel that it's 'just the way we are'. Luckily there are some brave people out there who aren't afraid to shine a light into this gloomy area. We CAN change and we NEED TO change if women are ever going to be truly accepted as equal in positions of power. So I leave with you a thought to consider, could you be one of these brave people?

WHAT NOW?

I am going to free you right now from any feeling of obligation to 'fix' the past or even the immediate present. Focus instead on doing better for the future. Play your part to create a future where a person is seen for their individual merits, not for their labels.

I believe that you will live the next level of change. Every generation of women and supportive men before you have taken the steps forward to allow women to thrive in a truly healthy career and now is the time to bring it all together and make it the new normal.

Support. Empathy. Strength. These are what you need to bring to every meeting, every team day, every group call to enable you and the women around you to thrive. This all counts for men too.

SUPPORT:

In any group situation you can either be IN the tribe, OUTSIDE the tribe or sitting in the MIDDLE, not sure if you belong or not. When you're IN the tribe, you have privilege. This privilege gives you power and a voice. You should always be looking to use that privilege to support and give space to those who are in the other two camps. Abusing that privilege to silence, belittle, ignore or dismiss others in that group has got us to where we are today with divided societies, run through with resentment, fear, hate and widespread discrimination on many levels. You can do better.

Take that to a work setting and undoubtedly you'll find yourself feeling different levels of belonging as you move between different teams and offices. As a white, educated, able-bodied, senior man you'll probably find that in most scenarios you are part of the tribe, part of the privilege. It's therefore your duty to support those in that meeting or team who you can see are outside of the tribe. This means giving your non-male, non-white, less able-bodied, more junior colleagues space to talk, validation of their opinions, credit for their ideas and actively having their back when they need you. **Supportive**

silence is no longer good enough. It's not good enough to stay quiet when a colleague brings a new idea to the table, only then to email them after to praise their creative problem-solving. Having that privilege means using it to actively and loudly support those who don't.

This applies equally for women. When you find yourself in a privileged position with a voice that is listened to, use it to support, encourage and lift others. Find solidarity amongst your colleagues and help each other to be heard and appreciated.

No matter how disadvantaged you feel in day-to-day life, you do have a tribe and you do have moments of power and influence: recognise these moments and use them wisely.

If you're looking for practical tips, the Obama administration in the USA hit the headlines in 2016 with its strategy for combatting the difficulties that women find when trying to be heard within the White House. In this challenging environment, women found themselves subject to such high degrees of unconscious bias and outright discrimination that they devised a specific approach between them to tackle it: they called it 'amplification'.

This technique is very simple and grounded in those notions of support and solidarity. The idea was that when one female colleague made a good point, if it was ignored then the other women in that meeting would repeat it and give credit back to the woman who had spoken. If it was still ignored, another woman did it again ... until there was some acknowledgement of what had been said. This was all done in the moment, within the setting of the meeting, not afterwards. They used their collective power to force the men in the room to openly listen to their ideas.

It's sad that strategies such as this were even needed and in 2021, fifteen years after this made news, I'd hope that it is now White House folklore rather than a daily requirement. It's important to appreciate just how recently this was all happening. The only way to push these behaviours into the history books is to never practise them in the first place. That's on you. Are you up for it?

THRIVE EXERCISE 8

Let's make all of this directly relevant. Have a think about the following questions:

1. When was the last time you saw female traits (shown by a man or a woman) belittled in some way or ignored at work (consensus, team working, empathy, doing something for the greater good, concern for others)? What happened? How did the people in the room respond?

2. Do you notice when a woman receives different treatment from a man at work? Has it happened to you (as a man or a woman)? How does it make you feel when you see that or if you can imagine it happening?

3. If you consider the culture of gender at your company, what words pop into your head? Is your company more heavily male or female and what impact does that have? What behaviours are praised and rewarded? Do policies favour one 'type' of person? How do senior managers behave in meetings towards those who are clearly not part of that 'tribe'?

4. What promises can you make around your own behaviours and attitudes to help move things forward? Could you speak to colleagues about the Obama Amplification technique if you feel that could be useful? Do you ever recruit or promote people? If so, how could you guarantee that there is no unconscious bias in that process? (TIP: asking HR to ensure that there is a mixed talent pool of CVs presented to you and then requesting that names be removed from the top of the CVs for first-round assessment is a good way to have a clean slate.)

5. Consider the generational make-up of your business. Has it ever caused any problems? Can you reflect on these problems with fresh eyes? Do you have different generations within your team? Could you do anything differently to minimise any friction and maximise people's contribution?

THRIVE: PRACTICAL TIPS

BE PROACTIVE AND ASSERTIVE

This doesn't mean that you need to be loud and overbearing, just that you find your own way to let people know what you want and what you're aiming for. Depending on your personality, you may find it hard to tell your manager or senior teams which type of role you'd like next or what area of the business you'd like to work in, so test out a few methods on friends or colleagues.

Of course, you need to be fairly clear in your head as to what it is you DO want and don't worry about it changing either – that's normal. The important point is that people can't help you if they don't know where you're trying to go. Women are traditionally worse at this than men. There can be a negative perception of women at work who are focused and driven (as we saw on page 181) so many prefer the 'telepathy' route where they rely on their managers picking up on hints and off-the-cuff comments. You can imagine that this route isn't the most reliable!

The only way you can be yourself at work and craft the individual career that you deserve is by letting people know what your goals are. Here are a few suggestions if you're not the 'straight out with it' sort of person:

★ **Appraisals.** If the standard process doesn't normally allow for 'future thinking' then let your manager know in advance that you'd like to add this onto the end.

★ If your awkwardness comes from the face-to-face side of this type of discussion, then write it down.

★ **Use your mentor or coach.** If they are within the organisation, then let these trusted people know which direction you'd like to take and let them help you.

★ **Ask for training or opportunities in a new area.** Your route doesn't have to be straight to a job! Show your interest and be pro-active.

★ **Use down-time** – on a work trip or if you're

travelling somewhere with a key colleague.
These moments of 'work but not work' are useful
to talk about the more personal or softer side of
our working life.

KEEP RE-ASSESSING

At the start of the book, we did some exploration of your
values and goals to help you develop an idea of your
palace. I mentioned at that point that your palace can
change shape, get extensions or even be replaced by
something else entirely – now it's time to re-enforce
that.

Life has a way of running off sometimes or taking
a turn that we could never have predicted. Perhaps
you have family problems, a new partner comes into
your life, or you discover a new skill that become
wildly passionate about – there can be a million
different reasons. The only way to try to keep your
career moving in a direction that continues to
suit you is to keep checking in with yourself and
assessing whether your current palace is still right
for you.

The amount of turbulence or unpredictability
in your life will alter the timings and frequency of
these 'check-ins'. My suggestion is that you do it at
least once a year. If you do it just before your annual
appraisal or a key development meeting with your
manager then you give yourself the best chance at
putting some new ideas on the table. But, as with
everything, find a way that suits your personality,
your job, your company and your lifestyle.

THRIVING IN YOUR FLOW

Ultimately thriving in your career will look different for everyone. As we've said, everyone is an individual so no two-people's journey down the river or their palaces will be the same, BUT we do need one another.

Thriving means that you are taking responsibility, showing empathy and being true to yourself. It won't always feel easy, there will definitely be challenges and uncertainties but when you're getting it right, you'll feel like you're in your flow. You'll have moments that just click, where everything makes sense, it's all easy and time seems to disappear without you even noticing. You could also call this, finding your 'mojo 'or being 'in the zone'. It's a real thing!

'Flow is the source code of ultimate human performance. You could also call it being in the zone or the technical term is an 'optimal state of consciousness' when we feel our best and we perform our best.'

This is the definition of Flow from Steven Kotler, one of the world's leading experts in human performance. It is a state that makes it feel like one action or decision is flowing naturally and effortlessly from the last. In this state of Flow, we become so focused that everything else disappears; time appears to slow down, our sense of awareness changes and we become completely absorbed. I'm sure you've felt it at some point, when you really get into something, and you are so focused that time passes without you realising and you produce something of really high quality.

This altered state of consciousness started being mentioned in papers and scientific works as early as 1871 by Albert Heim. By the 1970s, the 'Godfather of Flow Psychology', Mihàly Csìkszentmihàlyi, had turned that into 'Flow' following his global research study into positive psychology. He created definable and universal characteristics which can also be measured. He discovered that we are ALL biologically hard-wired to perform at our best in this state. More recently, Steven Kotler has written extensively on this topic and his work is fascinating.

I think of Flow as the tangible output of enjoying something. The exciting part about Flow is that it can be defined and measured, unlike 'enjoyment', so it can act as a reference point for both for you as an individual and for businesses as a metric for their employees.

Kotler tells us that Flow is fundamental to overall wellbeing and life satisfaction, so those who score the highest in flow measures, score the highest on life-satisfaction measures. Isn't that what we've been working towards throughout this whole book: using your career to help you gain life satisfaction?

Csìkszentmihàlyi found that workers in their Flow were more productive, got greater satisfaction from their work, set goals for themselves to increase their own capabilities and would even happily carry out work for which they weren't paid if it got them to a state of Flow. That sounds a lot like thriving to me!

To make that tangible, McKinsey carried out a fantastic piece of research on Flow in the workplace and found that senior executives found themselves to be 5x (or 500%!!) more effective when they were in a Flow state. That's the equivalent of being so productive on Monday that you can have Tuesday to Friday off! That's quite a win.

The point that ties flow back to everything we've been talking about in the book is that getting into a Flow-state only happens when you deeply connect to something. You need to be intellectually and emotionally operating at your best with a clear and meaningful purpose which you feel will make a difference. You can use our three Guiding Principles to get you there. By doing the groundwork that we've walked through in the book, you should be able to access that deep connection which leads you to Flow states.

WRAP UP

So how do you feel now we're almost at the end of the book? What has stuck? What have you changed? What will you do next?

My hope is that you have more self-confidence and awareness, a greater knowledge of some of what awaits you along your career journey and a few handy tips for your back pocket which you can use in your day-to-day working life.

Let's do a quick review:
We likened our career to a journey along a river in a boat. We could either take this journey purposefully and alert or in a more passive way. By setting a goal persona or creating a future version of ourselves, we took the purposeful approach. This helped us to make decisions, assess risks, learn, grow and

importantly, still have fun.

We had three Guiding Principles accompanying us throughout the journey. They have been our guiding lights time and time again, helping us navigate tricky new situations and to give us clarity in our own thinking. They were: Take Responsibility, Show Empathy and Know Yourself.

The ADAPT phase saw us through the first few months of a new career when everything is new and the learning curve is steep. We uncovered the best ways to set ourselves up in a business, building our network and listening carefully. We also benefitted from this time of low responsibility and demands to set some basic, healthy habits which would stand us in good stead for the long journey ahead of us, such as reflection, keeping a diary, moving our bodies regularly and goal setting. We learnt how to get the most out of our first challenges and the importance of practise and active learning.

We then moved onto the GROW stage of the journey. This was undoubtably the 'messiest' of all the stages. We witnessed continual challenges from the situations we found along the river which tested our internal resolve and stretched our skills. We also had a lot of fun at this point, as we settled into our role and the company and learnt to find excitement in the intensity of big pieces of work. It was at this stage that we practised how to manage negative scenarios such as saying 'no' and disagreeing with colleagues. We kept reviewing the importance of the three Guiding Principles as well as learning how to tackle difficult situations, make important decisions and take control of our own story.

Finally, we entered the THRIVE stage. Our

confidence and knowledge were at their height and we reflected on how best to use this 'power'. The opportunities to make an impact on the careers of others around you are plentiful and it is important to be conscious of your actions and the messages that you send out. Try to always be part of the force for positive change, working in a way that promotes equality, the power of individual thought and is supportive and encouraging of colleagues at all levels. This is also the point where we reached our goal persona or our palace. It's only a stopping-off point on our career journey but it's a significant marker which has taken a huge effort to realise, so we need to recognise our achievement and give ourselves the time to take it in and readjust.

By this point you should have amassed a healthy library of learnings, ideas, tips and positive habits which you will take with you as you return back to the boat and set off towards your next goal.

Thriving in your career doesn't have to be hard, but it does need to be conscious. It all starts with awareness and consciousness. Consciousness leads to thought, thought leads to intent, intent leads to action, action leads to change. We're all moving along our river, whether we like it or not, so let's make the best of it and make the best of ourselves.

You're ready now. Well-equipped to jump into your boat and look to the future with positivity.

Take responsibility, show empathy and know yourself.

ADAPT
GROW
THRIVE

FIND YOUR WINGS

Find Your Wings is a career coaching and mentoring business, specialising in supporting those who are in the early stages of their career or who are going through a career transition. We run programmes within businesses, taking employees through the ADAPT, GROW, THRIVE framework. For individuals, we offer personalised sessions when they need support moving to the next level in their career or those who are feeling career-stuck. We also work with sporting organisations and academies, supporting and teaching elite athletes about the transition out of elite sport and into their next career. We always have the same principles that underpin all of our work; the power of the individual and the need for a healthy career.

Please find out more about us at **www.findyourwings. co.uk** and Find Your Wings on LinkedIn or @ findyourwingsuk on Instagram and Facebook.

RECOMMENDATIONS AND REFERENCES

If you'd like to explore a little more about the themes we've covered in the book, here are some suggestions of places to start:

PODCASTS

The High Performance Podcast: Jake Humphrey and Prof. Damian Hughes interview people from all walks of life (primarily sports stars) who are regarded as 'high performing' and unpick their stories, motivations and advice for living a high-performance life. They have also just released a High Performance book.

Unlocking Us: Brené Brown. Very open and honest interviews talking about how to be true to yourself and understand your motivations as well as confronting some of society's biggest challenges.

Delicious Ways to Feel Better: Ella Mills. Founder of Deliciously Ella talks to some really interesting people on ways to get the best out of life and living in a happy, healthy and fulfilled way.

Feel Better, Live More: Dr Rangan Chatterjee. Interview style podcast covering all aspects of wellbeing, healthy living and thriving in life, with some unique and interesting guests.

BOOKS

Untamed: Glennon Doyle. A confronting and highly

engaging look at how society shapes us (specifically women) to the point at which we don't know what we want for ourselves anymore, we simply follow the expectations and stereotypes. She also has a podcast.

The Element; how finding your passion changes everything. Sir Ken Robinson. A fantastic practical guide to understanding the strength in doing what you love.

Green Lights: Matthew McConaughey. Stories and wisdom based on this Hollywood star's career and life principles.

REFERENCES TO STUDIES, WEBSITES AND BOOKS

In the order they are referenced in the book.

James Clear https://jamesclear.com

Honey and Mumford Learning Styles
https://www.youtube.com/watch?v=-92dIFiN_p8

Gretchen Rubin – The 4 Tendencies Quiz
https://quiz.gretchenrubin.com

The World Health Organisation information on Burn-out
https://www.who.int/news/item/28-05-2019-burn-out-an-occupational-phenomenon-international-classification-of-diseases

Stanford research: The Relationship Between Workplace Stressors and Mortality and Health Costs in the United States.
https://www.gsb.stanford.edu/faculty-research/publications/relationship-between-workplace-stressors-mortality-health-costs-united

The World Health Organization study on mental health in the workplace.
https://www.who.int/teams/mental-health-and-substance-use/promotion-prevention/mental-health-in-the-workplace

Harvard Business Review: Burnout Is About Your Workplace, Not Your People.
https://hbr.org/2019/12/burnout-is-about-your-

workplace-not-your-people

The Mayo Clinic list of burnout symptoms
https://www.mayoclinic.org/healthy-lifestyle/adult-
health/in-depth/burnout/art-20046642

**Harvard Business Review definition of Imposter
Syndrome.**
https://hbr.org/2008/05/overcoming-imposter-
syndrome

**Journal of General Internal Medicine paper on
'Treatment of Imposter Syndrome**
https://www.ncbi.nlm.nih.gov/pmc/articles/
PMC7174434/

**Medical News Today: Symptoms of Imposter
Syndrome**
https://www.medicalnewstoday.com/
articles/321730

**Qualitative Health Research paper Superwoman
Schema: African American Women's Views on
Stress, Strength, and Health**
https://www.ncbi.nlm.nih.gov/pmc/articles/
PMC3072704/

**One is the loneliest number McKinsey paper on
women in the workplace**
https://www.mckinsey.com/featured-insights/
gender-equality/one-is-the-loneliest-number?fbcl
id=IwAR3Ey2cGKEcGxaI7KaL3j3gm49XXOQ6YUJB
fc-oiU5PtvgWRzGSOG8YpZ6Y

NEOMA business school study
https://neoma-bs.com/

Independent newspaper article: Companies with women on boards perform better, study finds
https://www.independent.co.uk/news/uk/
home-news/women-company-boards-better-
performance-b1776181.html

Statistica: UK population by age
https://www.statista.com/statistics/281174/uk-
population-by-age/

The Leadership Styles of Women and Men: Eagly & Johannesen-Schmidt
https://is.muni.cz/el/phil/jaro2009/
PSB_516/6390561/the_leadership_styles_of_
women_and_men.pdf

Mary Ann Sieghart: Authority Gap
https://www.maryannsieghart.com/

Washington Post article on Amplification Strategy used in the White House
https://www.washingtonpost.com/news/
powerpost/wp/2016/10/25/how-a-white-house-
womens-office-strategy-went-viral/

'Father of Flow Psychology' Mihàly Csìkszentmihàlyi
https://www.youtube.com/
watch?v=fXIeFJCqsPs&t=225s

Positive Psychology, Mihàly Csìkszentmihàlyi
https://positivepsychology.com/mihaly-
csikszentmihalyi-father-of-flow/

Steven Kotler- Flow
https://www.stevenkotler.com/

McKinsey- Increasing the Meaning Quotient of Work
https://www.mckinsey.com/business-functions/
organization/our-insights/increasing-the-
meaning-quotient-of-work

ACKNOWLEDGEMENTS

Thanks go to those who helped bring this book to life:

Cover design and typesetting by Clare Baggaley.

Editing by Lisa Edwards.

Lightning Source UK Ltd.
Milton Keynes UK
UKHW022140261022
411123UK00018B/246